outlasting
the weather

selected & new poems
1994-2020

Friesen is a poet interested in what could be called the spiritual self ... a self, or poetic voice, grounded in clear observation of interior and exterior worlds, observation that makes itself visible in the poems.
—Maurice Mierau, from *How Mind and Body Move: the poetry of Patrick Friesen*

These fragments of a broken bowl are, indeed, much greater than the sum of their parts as they spur imaginal encounters not only with Friesen but with the scattered bits of the readers' self—each piece a new gesture to try on.
—Tim Lilburn, about *broken bowl*

Patrick Friesen sings us a city of music and memory, trains and terrors, bookstores and bridges. This is poetry that matters, poetry that calls us home and calls to the homelessness within us.
—Rosemary Sullivan, about *st. mary at main*

This (long) poem is a single penetrating take into the mind of the deeply disenfranchised. It seizes the margin as its centre and looks out from there, seeking the whole amid the broken. Always, Patrick Friesen is a poet who understands the necessity of, and insists upon, compassion.
—Sharon Thesen, about *short history of crazy bone*

... operating like yogic meditation, each breath-length line intends the literal inhalation and exhalation of meaning, blurring the frontier between physical and spiritual presence. Read aloud, these incantations transform the body from flesh-container to resonating musical organism.
—B. Glen Rotchin, *Globe and Mail*, about *the breath you take from the lord*

These unpunctuated, rhythmically complex poems, like jazz improvisations, are direct, immediate demonstrations of consciousness itself, how we make connections when the mind is open and aware of its entire history.
—George Amabile, about *jumping in the asylum*

outlasting
the weather

selected & new poems
1994-2020

patrick friesen

anvil
PRESS

For Marijke and Niko,
and our years together on Woodhaven Blvd.

Anvil Press Publishers Inc.
P.O. Box 3008, Main Post Office
Vancouver, B.C. V6B 3X5 Canada
www.anvilpress.com

Library and Archives Canada Cataloguing in Publication

Title: Outlasting the weather : selected & new poems, 1994-2020 / Patrick Friesen.
Other titles: Poems. Selections (2020)
Names: Friesen, Patrick, 1946- author.
Identifiers: Canadiana 20200290444 | ISBN 9781772141535 (softcover)
Classification: LCC PS8561.R496 A6 2020 | DDC C811/.54—dc23

Book design by Marijke Friesen
Represented in Canada by Publishers Group Canada
Distributed by Raincoast Books

The publisher gratefully acknowledges the financial assistance of the Canada Council for the Arts, the Canada Book Fund, and the Province of British Columbia through the B.C. Arts Council and the Book Publishing Tax Credit.

We acknowledge the financial support of the Government of Canada through the National Translation Program for Book Publishing for our translation activities.

PRINTED AND BOUND IN CANADA

*... and although nobody here really knows where they're going,
at the very same time nobody's lost ...*

("Hobo Jungle" by Robbie Robertson/The Band)

CONTENTS

Earth's Crude Gravities

jumping in the asylum

new work

A Broken Bowl

(1997)

a red-winged blackbird swaying on a reed in the ditch isn't very
    much among the broken glass and papers in greasy swamp
    water near kokomo road
but it's something a splash of blood a clear song a dream a
    memory it's something left behind forgotten something to
    hear in the morning's first light
a haunting a ghost this is how god and darwin dance this song
    of world this echo of northern lights and marsh
it's something entering your eyes and ears and skin an invisible
    tattoo a braille you feel and read but nothing revealed

it's me remembering how I saw the bird on its reed everything
    changes in the looking

always drums from the first heart beating to feet slapping hard
    earth the world over hands clapping the lost human finding
    a door the crack of a drum and entering earth's rhythm the
    cave of bones the path through the heart and beyond

the human infection spreading like music

I no longer sing the lullabies
no longer remember the melodies or the words

tongue confounded
the world scattered with grammar
we listen for the song

✠

*I'll say whatever you want that the river is rolling with heads I'll
say I've haunted highways with a blade I've sliced a fetus from its
womb and nailed a lizard to a tree I've lived in doorways heard lovers
through the walls I'll say whatever you want and it's the truth I'll say
whatever you want there are no fingerprints*

*I am the phone call you dread the filthy words the pain you hide
behind your pills I am your mother with her guilt your father with his
amnesia*

*I am your divinity the monster you dream at night I am who you want
to be free with a pocketful of gold I am your leader I speak from the
throne*

*this is not a confession this is a treatise on love this is your religion
your philosophy of life this is how you make truth*

I will tell you who I am I will tell you who you are

✦

*I am the law of the land the liturgy of wealth and power the law with
its underbelly and its shadows the law that fools you into civilization
the law that steals from the ancient people and proclaims the thieves
innocent the law the law that is the paperwork of the victors*

*and I am the other law that turns on the law tooth and claw the law
of human rage in its tatters and torn shoes the law of serf and slave
of the poor and the damaged and the brown and black the law of
the human spirit misshapen by law I am the hidden river bursting its
banks the law that passes understanding the law of the cornered rat
and the insane child beneath the bridge*

*I am the law that turns on the righteous and greedy and narrow I am
the law that puts a blade into the hand of the broken and the sick and
hopeless I am the law that strings up the tyrant and becomes the new
one*

*everywhere I am the law everywhere and I favour none all will die
beneath the law judged judged judged*

this century's poems
conjuring words
names and places
sarajevo
auschwitz
soweto
these incantations
like train cars clicking by
or convoys rolling through rubble
dubrovnik
mogadishu
hiroshima
like parachutes drifting through a summer sky
or fireworks
or a million footsteps
solovetzki
watts
kahnawake
a million footsteps
leading to the river
the baptism
kings and princes on the barge
dancing with the whores
listening to water music
and playing die

no salvation
we just dig ourselves deeper
with each attempt
there is only this
walking and crawling and standing still
there is only this victim this murder
there is the human hand on a shovel
digging for clues

we are romans with our headaches and anxiety we are a trivial
people brutish and blind
we are romans standing in sewage craving the law and God
with his scalene triangle
senators and patricians spread their greed and flash to the eager
plebs and we run to the arena
there is murder in the streets hostages and spectators strippers
become naked again and again
there is such a thirst for another city unquenchable a thirst for
some rich city a walled place of desire
but all cities are rome the boutiques and love shops and the
buildings of law and order

we are romans with our senators our laws and our shabby gods
we worship everything nothing is sacred

the bronze horseman rides alone
in his terrible intelligence
once more through mist and rain
back to the northern bog

this is how you build a city
on the bones of ghosts
you wrench a civilization
out of the silences of history

this is how you satiate kings
how you obey the mob
you fashion paradise with terror
and worship angels in the beast

a monk on fire ... the serenity and rage ... not a sacrifice, really,
a signal, a gesture ... the rage of flames wrapping themselves
around him, the absolute control and rage of flames flaying
him alive without thought or intent, only the duty to burn and
feed, wrapping themselves around him like a saffron robe, his
second skin ...

the horrible serenity of the human machine without desire ...

a transfiguration ...

from estrus to romance
from romance to coltrane
man and woman
contending in the rain

ah love
byzantine exaltation
all icons and worship
an addiction to paradise
and the end of time
the grease of serotonin
slippery in the brain

then turn around
and a numbing despair
the machine collapsed
into nuts and bolts and pain
and no sense anywhere
the music broken
and time dragging its ass
across a field of shattered glass

two of us
walking in the rain
sodden clothes
clinging to these bodies
of skin and brain and heart
and all the other parts
lust and love
the betrayal
and the companion you've always dreamed

from estrus to romance
what a waltz
how the earth accumulates
its wars and fossils
how we keep digging them up
and falling in love

the words to a lullabye keep recurring
the clicking of train wheels
old casey and the orange blossom special
on its way to the end of the line

swing the pick
tote that load

old songs at memory's edge
the old moon in the new moon's arms
a dead knight beneath his shield

the words that sang me to sleep
on the tip of my tongue
and me dreaming in the quarry
an endless line of shuffling figures
trains lumbering by
swollen with freight
and nothing but the clicking of wheels

✦

*I am malory the rapist imaginer of romance and chivalry inventor of
the world you play at you will find me beneath the bridge with a blade
in hand show me your paltry coins or I will run you through*

*I am torquemada your personal confessor I will guide you to heaven
I am the duke of alva let me invite you to holocaust everyone will be
there*

*I am savanarola and john calvin come warm yourself at my fire we'll
talk about your doubts I'm sure I have an answer*

*I am marco polo I am prester john I've been everywhere and I come
from nowhere that you know I could tell you things you would never
believe so I tell you things you will believe I'm waiting for you at the
end of your quest*

a dish
stone steps
a dancer

scattered in grass
buried in deserts
these things of man and woman
an obsidian blade
a painted wall
these things
made us gods
in our own right

an ancient breastbone
ribs
held a fire
and let go
the contagious heart

spreading
through valleys
of the rift
the serengeti
himalayas

a disease
to make us gods
beasts in love
and war
turning to watch
the infected sky

and world going down
around us

✦

wordless they emerge from forest and desert
clothed in the steaming skins of animals
dancing slowly into an eyeless fury

only memory can offer such rage
children broken on the wheel
their tents slashed open to the sky

going down
earth's diary
its broken bowl
and ashes

going down
through shell and leaf
and debris
to initials on the stairs

going down
the ladder
breaking into
an empty house

going down
to the world's mouth
for an echo
of the first orphan

going down
in an easy death
a raw word
in the star's cave

this place of evidence

laid out bones
and the stone seeds of wreaths

the debris of home
a broken bowl
a doorstone

and a stick
with carved shapes
a calendar
or worship
a poem

this place
where a woman understood
soil and sun and moon
and stood back

someone saying
with hands
and stuttering tongue

a man turning
to look back
where he was

becoming strangers

the last two frames
from nate saint's camera
found in the curaray

two naked women
on the beach
the curaray running
behind them
the younger one
holds a drink
and a cloth
in front of her breasts
her left leg lifted
and inclined inward
to hide her pubic hair

water has bled
like a black flame
into the next frame
and like a black flame
burned
up the middle of the frame
corroding the women
from the scene
in the background
around the black flame
trees
and the river

and there
where desert meets the city
in a shantytown
where squalor defines our wealth
there
where God lies beneath rubble
where the bowl is broken
there
a moment we might miss
a glance
a caressing hand

you never know

at the river's edge
you can dream
of the dancer

the bearded savior
disappearing into the rain

you can remember
old steps
and the human gesture

a hand waving

what startles you
is the imp
in the underbrush
doubled-over
with laughter

no
there is no easy word
for this
how we hear
for a moment
then go deaf

imagining whispers
at the river's edge

a family
gathering
in the open
and predators
slipping
through the grass

one of us
finding a way
to the end of the world
baffled there
and turning back
toward the story

a hand waving farewell
and the laughter
time and again

sometimes
you can hear the howling of their dogs
bells and the soughing wind

moving along the way
by foot or horseback

with their golden bracelets
walking past wall and plough

in long grass
they pitch their black tents
and the story begins again

st. mary at main
(1998)

the angel wakes

I know the light's on
all night at esther's
and lerner and fournier
are playing at sunstone
I know dave's bending
notes at times change

and the city lives
catching its breath
as towers fall away
and false Gods
shut their gobs

donahue's on corydon
talking with time
outside heaven
don and carol
on their evening walk
stop at nucci's
who knows what characters
carol's harbouring
mcmanus in the west end
shaping a few of his own

the angel wakes
from a troubled sleep
stirring the city alive
into a night of prayer
and dance

I know the lights on
all night in the north end
that music leaks
through two or three doors
where they're gathered
and the wind blows long
down the avenue

midtown bridge

I don't know why this comes back to me
it was midnight in may 1967
and I was standing on the midtown bridge
throwing money into the assiniboine
$200 it was a test a question of discipline
what comes back is the soft air that night
the liquid ripple of water I could hardly see
dark and silver and beckoning
I think I threw the money in lieu of myself
that was a necessary consideration those days
and across two rivers the beacon of the neon cross
what comes back is the loosening of my shoulders
my body relaxing into an illusion of freedom
thinking for the moment an illusion is as good as the real thing
and walking home with a light step and an empty pocket
not sure now any of this happened
the bridge the river I remember
the rest money and life all a story
long gone fluttering through air

this is how the streets are wired

donahue on corydon
dressed with elegance
his hair grey past his gifts
eyes round like a spooked horse
he's got rent to raise
and living on cucumbers and water
I'm wishing he could tune up
right there on the sidewalk
but he's pawned his guitar
and I miss his irish tenor

what is it some spirits do with their grace?
resisting the full circle
like they can't handle too much
the wiring's all wrong
and they've electricity sparking off their hands
their hair on fire their eyes borrowed from a crazy dream

and others drink their way out of bodies
burning through to the smoke of soul
and always in the morning
crumpled once more in their charred flesh
the romance long gone
some find words in talk or the keyboard
slithering out of their skins and hunger
into the night's beauty
golden bodies adrift until morning
with the scrawl to answer for
the utter risk the scratchings in the light of day

and donahue is at the heart of this city
even without his guitar
and his voice vanishing
he's come through
to name the streets he walks
his conversations at intersections
touching the city like a current
this is how the streets are wired

marlene dietrich didn't live here

marlene dietrich didn't live here
edith piaf or lotte lenya
nothing that well-dressed and world-weary
I never saw modigliani asleep on the boulevard
an empty bottle and a shabby suit
the man could charm a pigeon
didn't see him the night he walked all night
down parisian streets with akhmatova
just saw photographs of her various rooms
and his drawing in the background
an elegance on bare soviet walls
he didn't make love in this city
no shows at the plug in gallery

no ottoline morrell no garsington
and no jacques brel what a shame
no giacometti no camus or cocteau
the endlessness of european names
smothering their cities and cafés
with delicacies pomposity and delights
loaves of french bread and airie confections
play and more play so many years of pretending
and we're just beginning

homeless

we are ophelias and lears
we are starlings and purple strife
beautiful in our homelessness
a white wind from another land
the falling seeds of manna
we are the heroes of our imagination
dreaming winnipeg where the rivers meet
and building our stage there

come now that we live here
it is long time we turn
and work our way into other imaginations
heroes become brutal
grimacing in their awful masks
heroes are blind missionaries
martyrs to what they no longer see
and executioners of what they never saw

we are lears on the plains
storms around our mad decisions
we are orphans
wandering ever further from home
a trail of shoes behind us
old clothes and masks
barefoot finally on the stage
with nothing to say

st. michael and all angels

living this heart attack of a life on these streets tonight passing
    st. michael and all angels church
stone and low beneath dark trees almost an outpost a barracks a
    corner of england famous and mildewed
high anglican dust and elegance and thomas hardy in the shade
    with angel clare and eustachia vye

a ghost on the street corner and the beautiful voices of traherne
    and vaughan and herbert
wandering through heaths kings and daughters and barefoot
    tinkers buried in barrows
webster's genius the howl of a heavy note his unlidded eyes
    looking to the darkness within

all the words and rhythms are rain or wind a common book of
    prayer or john donne from the pulpit
it's what we speak here on most of these streets at least a
    bastard child with too many words
and the ghost stands there with his tuxedo wilting at the sleeves
    with the smell of rose water and daffodils

trains

at night
I tell time by trains
a distant diesel
the rumble of its wheels
from a mile away
across the assiniboine
through my window
I tell time
once in a while
the european engine
sixteen coaches
ghosting through the city
in the utter dark
I tell time
in the station
waiting for word
from away

a train is the distance grief travels
singlehearted and relentless
the weight of horizon
on a standing man
it is forgotten terrain
shifting from birth to birth
a train never comes around
it returns the way it went

trains pass
through the city's sleep
being dreamed
like rivers

like memory
with its freight
I tell time by trains
old stories riding the rod
through the night

thorkkelson glass

my friend paul says
once you see the light of greece
you understand its philosophers
he's from nafplion
and swears by its sky
our light is clear
thorkkelson glass
with blue clouds shimmering inside
and bare branches scratching the horizon
with their calligraphy
our light is not human
not shaped not interpreted
this is a cool light
a blue silk umbrella
arching over the city
as light as whispers
in the tent of the world

ellice avenue

among the used furniture shops italian clubs laundromats and
    german corner groceries two wandering ghosts
my two-year-old daughter riding high on my shoulders her fists
    clutching my hair my hands loosely circle her ankles
1975's sun slanting into my squinting eyes her bare legs brown
    and round with power
my dear it's twenty years done and you're back in this city and
    it feels like I'm on my way gone

it's easy to let nostalgia seep in a man's life disappearing his
    daughter almost his age now
you know what I mean how time differs for them so much
    faster for him than it was so much brighter
the way a photograph fades to brilliance a woman's dark hair
    flaring to white fire around her face
it's so easy to vanish into memory slipping from body into mind
    into thin air into light

it's a still-life those blocks a frozen blur of motion us walking
    through our lives
the body remembers the heat the summer swish of traffic the
    sounds of portuguese and german
the body is a memory of landscapes europe and asia gutturals
    and sibilant whispers of history
an old man with his medals maria at the window her nose
    flattened to the glass

all is flesh and the shadow I used to be sloughed skin on sticks
    following me around
there's eternity a rotten concept if ever the blackbird in the
    marsh as my soul

feathered and small-boned on a cattail and swaying in a slow
    northern wind
doesn't matter marijke because it's enough to be here in the
    improbability of this world

and we're not long for it no one is maria disappears from her
    window the old man already forgotten
they still sell used furniture they play cards in the clubs but the
    corner store is vietnamese
brides still stand on the top steps of their porches waiting for
    the cameras to flash
my shoulders have rounded since 75 but I still feel your fine
    ankles in my hands

quick and dark as a crow

sturgeon creek's high tonight
and the moon is cold
the rain across the water
wants to be snow

driving into the heart of the city
to the times change blues bar
to find the wildness I've been
another side to the road
going blind with song
son house and muddy waters
coming through like strays
how they let themselves go
and I've been blind before
I know how it goes
feeling my way
quick and dark as a crow

the harmonica wailing
a blowing wind
then sliding low
as a bellering hound
there's thunder in the fields
and crickets beneath the porch
someone walking out of town
there are mirages on the road

strange this music
that's been traveling so long
it's got feet without a home
feels like sorrow
that hardly remembers
where it came from
and doesn't know where it's going

just moaning and growling
here in this city
unquiet spirits from the delta
shuffling down the street
bleeding dark blood
from their old wound
in the morning they're gone

there's nothing but
a quiet sunday street
and that muffled drumbeat
rising at the forks
talking skin
and slow dragging feet
there's nothing but
a ghost dance
where the rivers meet

flood

we know it will come rolling along like rumours from the south
word of mouth you stop and hold your breath to listen and
think you hear it like gossip or stories a distant rumble of
water but there's only a gentle wind playing with the silence
we know it will come like a forgotten promise we wait
stunned in a dream looking for signs of miracle looking for
something we can do we build walls around our houses and
we wait and wait and wait
we know it will come blood flowing in our veins like swelling
rivers the earth our body we melt into it with our anxieties
we return to the earth and its ways stripped of culture and
sophistication standing with hands at our sides

what are we? old questions rise with the water our strangeness
on earth our separation and our dominion waters rise and
nudge us toward memory we shrug it off but fear seeps
through something unnamed and concealed
what have we done? the red river is rolling toward us in disorder
and disease an impending judgement the river spreading
across fields a distant glitter of light relentlessly surrounding
us

and then it arrives cresting against our bulwarks all bloated and
bitter with its cargo of beasts carrying our filth and the death
of factories bones rolling in the water our history haunting
us the drownings the sunken ships
it rolls through towns and cities a violent baptism a punishment
of the planet houses and sheds tilting downstream trees
uprooted civilization a thin wall of sandbags and the
desperation of the human animal with its reason its cunning
and prayer

the river rolling through our world of words and architecture
bursting through laws and assumptions

in the end it's a story told by an old man on a bench
remembering and waiting for his end it's biblical because we
name it this story of dogged restlessness
in the end we are displaced so easily not a judgement not a
punishment but simply the way the earth moves and we
scratch at the surface leaving our marks and our bones
in the end no one walks on water we claim our property and
close our eyes in sleep the river returns to its narrow bed and
waits

place louis riel

she is all beautiful naked at the window the gauzy curtains
    around her as she gazes across the city
she watches a slow train slip the snowy banks of the river the
    basilica open to the stars
she has blessed this room with her scent the soul of her
    trembling with fine strength
she is elegance in a tough city the care with which she moves
    through the world

from the window you can see the city open out to the prairie
    steel rails vanishing
the dawson trail with its ghosts and whisky jacks almost lost
    beneath snow
madame gaboury and the grey nuns and hanged louis buried
    across the river
but here this woman in the flesh what has always been with us a
    lover and a ghost

at night when muscles sleep when the rough hand lies on white
    cotton sheets
in the dark after the day's deals when love and rage fester
    behind the drapes
she moves through the streets breathing for us and making
    angels in the snow
she calls on what's best in us touching the frost at our windows
    and the shoe at the door

incense for the lord

running late with the blue torpedo in my blood looking for
    sleep for something to recall
that's how it goes here in st. james the sun long down and birds
    asleep in the trees
straying toward the garden the old woman still stooped there
    among the peas her hands adrift
it's an irish temptation this borderland where the flesh goes up
    in smoke an incense for the lord

longing for flight this dead weight unshackled for the night
    diving off a stone wall
it's my house foundering here on woodhaven a husk my bones
    gone to ground skinned and quick
dreaming like the shakes thin walls breached to that terrain I've
    come from and return to when I can
that's how it is with the body I adore it its gates and windows
    sprung open I love to leave

breathing in the serene flame of the body's ardour flesh on fire
    with its hunger and thirst
it's the lord moving in mysterious ways writhing through the
    throes of creation
exhaling like death the breath funnelling out to its end the blue
    torpedo riding home
that's how it goes here in this room the body's smell
    everywhere its words and convulsions

st. mary at main

walking through the city's terrain
its grids and maps
its money and electricity
walking toward times change
and bev's smile at the door

I love to sit at the window
watching the trains go by
quarter moon hanging there
like a broken clock
and I've got the time

isaac's rolling a mellow cigarette
blues woven into the tension of his hands
always playing beneath what he feels
batting a slow eye as he reaches back

dave's feeling his way
through the night
his silver guitar
strung with dark strings

the city getting drunk
on saturday night
the city teetering
between savagery and bliss
there's so much
to drink away
so much to drink toward
everyone looking for good news
trying to break through

the blue glass of heaven
there's all that love
on the streets
you can see it brawl
its way into forgetfulness

main street's so thirsty
no one gets enough
dreaming toward sunday morning
the hungry ones
hoping for manna
the power and the glory
amen and selah
the loners who have seen god
and gone poor

and there's no way for the nomad
the paths have all been paved
and it's the separation
of heart and brain
and everyone's insane
shadows beneath streetlamps
bodies lurching through doorways
we're all silhouettes in the window
trying to make ends meet
body and soul

as they say
keeping the wolf from the door
the blues at 1 a.m.
dave squinting beneath his cap

watching everything
the shuffle
everyone a step closer
or farther from god
home for a moment
in the song
and the voice's desire
the world here
at st. mary at main
a train ghosting by
and the brakeman looking back

dawn

streetlamp leaning
into the early morning's light
buckled pavement
and broken glass

last night's commerce
litters wellington
and bannatyne
doorways lit
by the sun

city's going down

collapsing
into its own memory

empty streets
and the fluttering wings
of the 6 a.m. angel
ascending

blow wind blow

the breath you take
from the lord
(2002)

I.

late afternoon sun blazes off birch trees and you're caught by a
    clearing where you were born
you know that light like you know breath like you know the
    unnamed earth around you
you remember how the mind moved rustling like a small
    animal in underbrush skittering among the leaves

there is room for sadness here this is the place where a boy
    understands more than he knows
barbed wire and wild roses the tangle of a man's life how he
    encounters himself looking back
a hand on the bark of a poplar eyes still wondering at
    everything the flash of a wing the strike

you know how it works how you have to stand still letting the
    light climb up your trunk
you have to forget most things human this is not a place where
    anything has happened
you are a man you don't know how else to say it you are a man
    who has always sought god

there is a kind of indifference here hushed and slow it doesn't
    matter what you've been
it doesn't matter what you know you are almost a child here
    neither lost nor found not making strange
there is nothing you owe but the words you come to and those
    words are your seal

there is room for a mind between the high prairie sky and this
   scrappy undergrowth
how the air stirs shifting from one silence to another something
   about to happen
bare thickets in the fall a last pale rain arriving the way distant
   thunder hollows out the afternoon

the boy learns to stand among the trees a kind of listening at
   the edge of things
it's the step in that kills the man released into the open helpless
   and abandoned
if it wasn't for the rain who could live through the clearing if it
   wasn't for that mercy?

2.

a slant of light that kind of silver light among the poplars that
    kind of sudden silence
you slow as you approach or it arrives a moment you might
    have dreamed or not
that kind of light stops your breath with fear you stand thin
    behind the last tree
staring at an emptiness filled with spear grass thistles and the
    end of world
so much missing there almost everything you know in the
    darkness of your memory

there is nothing so empty so quiet and becalmed in heat and
    doldrums and shivering at the edge
like the fox or deer you don't enter the field you gaze through
    the leaves and circle
you can't throw your life away you can't enter the abandon you
    long for can you?
a snake slides from a stone pile the hawk's shadow passing and
    clouds wavering in grass
you stalk the lit heart of earth slipping through scrub brush
    beneath the shimmer of leaves

is this disorder this stillness this clearing that shines like an eye
    this ring of bones?
you are a child always you are a child here baffled and waiting
    for the wind
you freeze as if you've been seen you don't breathe all you hear
    is the pulse in your ear
no it is something colder than childhood something
    unremembered and relentless
home ground where you learn to speak in two voices where
    you are never at home

staring clarity the heart diminished to a fist how wind sweeps
    down from a far cold place
there is nothing for this emptiness this moment where nothing
    is and your eyes want to close from seeing
you can still smell the grease of birth on your arms your legs
    the grease of your first birth
and you smell death that old smell of empty places quick as air
    across your face
but you stand looking a faithless man standing his ground at the
    edge of the clearing

3.

when god tears at your heart or you think that's it you want
  that to be it angels perhaps or demons
when you need something to shape suffering something to hold
  it with intention

when the night deepens and you stand slow and waiting for
  your eyes to take in the trees
when you make your way through deadfall scraping your arms
  on the knuckles of a poplar

when the clearing flares with light the moon's brilliance
  carefully milking the thistle
when the stone pile glistens and cools sun's heat rising into the
  lowering sky

when nothing my god happens nothing in the vastness of your
  small rash living
when you have to laugh at the end of yourself at the god you
  think you've reached

when you crouch at a cold bethlehem as a constellation wheels
  across the clearing
when the offering you brought lies scattered at your feet and
  the only gift a broken heart

when you watch as you always have from the edge suddenly
  aware something breathes behind you
when you fear the darkness of bush the animal there but no
  safety in the clearing

when you find the body of the child struck down in its ecstasy
of light and lamentation
when you step into the barefoot prayer at least when you pass
into the open night

4.

this is a precise place on your grandfather's farm a hard place by
    that you mean you stumbled on it
and it is hard with stones the brown grass spare and sharp its
    breath is harsh
this place holds nothing else a taut empty womb which birth
    has long abandoned

you surround the clearing with your stealth something more
    than animal something stray
gazing across you see where you were and will be again as you
    move around the world
there is nothing to lose anymore but you don't believe that as
    your eyes search for what is lost

grandfather knew this place it's where he dragged the bones of
    his dead animals
you hear his gruff voice the coarse words that urged the horses
    in their ringing harness
it's a language that wastes neither time nor tenderness but
    holds what a gaunt man knows of love

yes the horses grazed here their brown hides twitching with
    flies and the full smell of their lives
you watched them all afternoon slowly cropping their way to
    the heart of the clearing
standing there coppery in the sun long heads raised to the wind
    listening to you move

and you wonder who hauled their carcasses later what voice
    called out that afternoon
the farm sinking like a ship into the memory of an old man
    toothless before his god
just the language is left what you learned about words meant
    beneath meaning

and how he strode into the clearing reins in hand turning his
    horses to release the load
how he disappeared again into the trees all lean and bone and
    calloused hands
how his voice faded the air closing behind him and you swung
    back into the silence

5.

bones in the clearing and leaves turning in july this is the still
    month without rain
this is when you can hear the dog in the distance and you know
    he's coming for you
you are a boy and your smell hardly brushes the grass but the
    dog remembers

within your grandfather's rooted smell his hands on stone his
    sweat on a fence
his bleak years the way everything disappeared the way
    everything happened again
within the smell of one man's grasp reins handles and latches a
    woman's hair

within grandmother's death the smell of a million deaths the
    smell of snow on air
november bearing down grey as iron bands of breath from
    horses among bare trees
within the smell of the house blowing from an open door
    windows black with night

within the smell of your father's life his torn clothes and pride
    the smell of fresh-sawn planks
bending over his shirt with needle and thread and clearing his
    throat with a quiet cough
within the smell of sen sens the voice of a man in song his good
    eye on the notes

your small smell and the dog on your trail this is the place
    where you listen
this is the place to be alone where entrails vanish beneath the
    crow's clear eye
your smell is faint but the dog knows it and here leaning against
    the birch you know it too

6.

this is not nature this scrub and thistle this clearing this is
    human this is broken land
this is war the brain this is the brilliant mind in love with
    horizons and desolation
the bones of barney and prince a rusting harrow in the weeds
    the ghost of a farmer at the plough
you hold brown photographs and a testament standing there
    among the columbines

all the things of god how they seduce you god within the thing
    you touch with your tongue
and you have to kill temptation don't you turn your back to it
    the world inside god
but it's hard killing god barefoot in the grass the long limbs of
    him the reach of him
and you can't the smell of him everywhere his spoor you track
    it in the night

something tore open this clearing some axe some plough but
    something more
before the shelterbelt before the dawson trail before the trails
    beneath the trail
first the hand fingerbones palm and heel then everything else
    the brain's cul de sac
dream broke open and bled the long line of the dream from
    ravines and foot broke the path

a killdeer's shrill cry calling rain its thin brown wings angling
    into flight this you know
the storm you weathered was nothing a little thunder lightning
    and it passed

always you've stood here watching and wanting to enter but
    waiting for a call
you've learned to answer no it's how you've managed to live
    love and refusal

it's something you know patience what you are like that bloody
    bird bowing the cattail
but the moment comes when you leave nothing left but the
    swaying reed
the moment arrives when you concede pride of thought the
    arrogance of belief
you want god you mean mother and father you think you hold
    love in your steadfast arms

lies you don't know what you want what it means all you know
    is your crouching
your hand reaching supplicant and you're squinting blue-eyed
    against the only light
you are an idiot your mouth gaping your arms aching with
    work you are almost invisible
the clearing is a suicide the mirror you want to smash and a
    mirage to dive into

you can't name god trying to live outside of that the cheap
    mechanics of civilization
this place is not nature the hand has touched it but the hand has
    done worse elsewhere
the idea the pattern sheer greed puts an end to things the
    process of eye mind and act
and you can't name that either your house leaning around its
    rotting timbers

so you return to the clearing the silent dog off its leash and it's a
    quick step into family
you've heard the tales of voyage and grief you've read the
    journals the details of gardens
you stand back to see you stand back for the necessary breath
    you stand back for what can't be named
you've always worshipped in your anger in your distances in
    your utter ignorance

15.

rain comes down that sparse night rain in october you feel the
    sad rhythm of fall
not sad not quite a whispering among the leaves as if something
    might be alive

your mother playing *träumerei* on the piano and singing you
    into dream with *wiegenlied*
you remember that desire to sing to meet the need in her voice
    to find the words

it's a trap of course there's not a damned thing you can do but
    reach for the notes
what you want is to sing anonymously you want to sing as if
    you are the voice of the world

now you listen to *peace piece* thinking it's rain on the leaves rain
    inside your head
thinking there's not a false note there's no presence outside the
    playing and no player

you imagine his hands hovering over the keyboard anticipation
    what is held back
and what is released his fingers thinking to the bottom of the
    key what can't be sustained

yes it's rain on poplar leaves on a wooden bench rain on a shed's
    tin roof those variations
it's a falling of rain and you're inside it and no it's not his song
    it's never his song

and this touches on what matters doesn't it not how you think
    about the clearing but how you enter
this is about how you live here your mind moving without
    thought in this home

17.

crisp air cuts into your lungs long shadows of aspen on lit snow
    not much is this still
not much speaks as well about you and you feel home in this
    thin wintry night
the owl watches and the hour shifts into the next you pause like
    breath on air

you love winter light at night the clearing cold and starry and
    far from earth
no need to raise your hand against the sun and your eyes widen
    to take everything in
you find nothing in too much light nothing but obscurity
    nothing but the thought of god

you pick your way through deadfall plunging sometimes to
    your knees listening to your breath
when you stop and stand you hear the blood flowing through
    your body's terrain
how can you be so sunken into earth and hardly on it at all or is
    it world you hardly know?

you don't see the wind rise but you hear it soughing through
    black spruce near the frozen slough
it's an old sigh that moves through you with everything you've
    known and what you can't
it is the groan of leaving of moving among bare trees toward
    what's open what's there

when you enter the clearing you are caught a stark animal
   tracked in the snow
you see only the dark circumference of the unbroken circle
   you've come from
you are wild in the bright snare laughing in this ambush this
   calm and fatal release

19.

nothing is saved and love lives only today in the hunger of your
    eager eyes

the child who carries you for a while the lover you've finally
    found to hold these days with you

for god men willingly murder men it has been so for long a
    crease perhaps in the circle of the brain

for god men would hasten the world to their paradise for god
    men build their babel

some days you smell exhaust drifting through the trees it settles
    on the columbine

you hear the town siren at supper the workers walking home
    and the machine runs on

the town believes so hard they worship themselves thin and
    hardly anyone reaches for the wine

you fall asleep at the edge of the clearing when you wake snow
    has fallen for a million years

you have grown young and ancient you rise in the still air your
    breath in clouds before you

the shadow of a man beneath the moon struggling through the
    snow and night

26.

barefoot jesus coughing in the rain in samaria no one good in
    sight and the figs not ripe
you imagine a fever and you imagine his thought sometimes
    you almost know what he saw

a man stumbles to the water to wash his blind eyes and opens
    them to an old world
does he hear a sparrow darting through air or does he enter
    darkness once again?

you love the story of assisi preaching to the birds calling on
    them to sing praises to the lord
and they sang their wings fluttering the songbirds sang but you
    wonder where the hawk flew

you lose the world over and over love is unruly the disorder that
    brings good it can it can
it's what you hold here your children your lover death in your
    heart it's possible

who is it you hear speak as you speak sing as you sing what
    voices live in you?
a harsh call in the clearing and that breath that deep breath you
    take from the lord

october poem

lost in itself a cat stretches on the porch no quickness left it
    gazes across the strewn lawn turns slumping back to sleep
the air is thick with golden light droning bees slow and drunk
    lifting heavily from apples oozing on the ground
everything's drying with fullness the second hand crawling
    around the clock a ball game drifting through the radio
a barefoot girl in the garden sprawls among roots and withered
    rhubarb weaving a rope of reeds

it's a satiated month people wander through cemeteries reading
    stones and entering old stories
we begin to leave the place we've lived and move into time
    going blind as moles in the dark
the last things of summer still before us but utterly changed a
    breeze suddenly filled with shivers
a boy hangs onto the silence of the willow his memories
    shifting to dream as his eyes look in

we've gathered the riches of earth in our aprons and baskets we
    have filled our cellars against the long winter
we pause like everyone before us has ever paused the hunch of
    death in our bones
this has happened forever this moment when we know what we
    are and where we've come from
october flows in our veins besotted we look back thankful and
    hesitant in our remembering

imagining mother and child who left their footprints long
    before history glancing at the sky
the chance and choice of seasons and weather the way almost
    nothing happens as intended
the ambiguity of our spirit clear or possessed a slender arm in a
    dance or the brain's brutality
we work through the year's blackberries and bramble through
    the hours toward evening

for a moment there is no need in our bodies though something
    haunts us as night absorbs day
walking beneath the streetlights in the clatter of acorns on a
    shed's tin roof we reach out to hold hands
this isn't romance or chivalry we reach out of loneliness bare
    trees creaking with the age
we are this species in debt to the earth facing the hunger and
    cold with our companions

november poem

november's ankle-deep in snow working its way along the
    railroad toward a midnight sun
november fills with flurries so soft they tickle the back of your
    bare hand and catch on your lashes
early november is the pause between seasons between centuries
    when we look back with hope forward in fear
how do we approach the end of things now this century how
    do we say farewell in a blizzard?

the century began with bayonets and dancers nijinsky
    descending heavily to the killing floor no longer embraced by
    air
the snow and blood of a century moving so swiftly beneath its
    burden the weight of machine and thought
he looked for another kind of grace heavy boots and treading a
    desperate game of fox and goose
nijinsky dancing in the asylum his own and the world's the last
    home of lost memory

november is a russian month with its thistle bass and soprano
    the deep solace of voices surrendering to a sundered time
ancient peasants in their knowing ignorance all scythe and time
    gobbing on their floors and crossing themselves
the spent casings of shells like seeds beneath first snow winter
    wheat and a promise of hunger
and they sing of sorrow and bandits and wandering the liturgy
    of the outcast and the lover of eternity

the century turns in november with its turmoil and an eye on
    january cold and hard and new
nijinsky dreamed this death giving way to gravity and trying
    one last time to shape it human
but human is a trickster's shape clever and greedy for bullets
    greedy for paradise
the dancer falls in the snow frozen feet in rags and eyes on the
    sun that won't go down

flurries fly in november across the world a russian choir sings of
    easter and christmas just ahead
those voices hold much but we hardly hear them the world's
    radio so very loud
the railroad's buried the crosses of war leaning into the wind
    the wars forgotten in monuments
and the machines the machines rumble on the highways we
    think they're ready for the blizzard

december poem

jello's hardening on the porch christmas punch cooling in a drift
    the shadow of a fox steps lightly behind a hedge
who's that singing *hark the herald angels sing* off-key in the pale
    light falling from the kitchen window?
it's the barber with a comb in his back pocket the town fool and
    henry with his hohner harmonica
they've forgotten words and no song book but it doesn't matter
    they haven't all forgotten the same ones

henry's hammering at the door the harmonica frozen to his lips
    and he stumbles in to thaw it off
the barber with his bowl haircut reaches for walnuts and cracks
    them between his splintered teeth
there's talk of blizzards and 1934 or was it 43 the war rations the
    good old days
and henry with blood on his teeth wonders if he can have
    another mandarin orange

I'm remembering the fox caught her in the corner of my eye
    and I go out to find her
there is no distance like december's distance how far across the
    field how far to the star of the east
the clarity of air takes my breath the fool's shadow stretching
    from the window across the white lawn
there's no fox can't find her prints a ghost of christmas past and
    I unplug the car for a drive

skidding down #12 past akron where father was born past
    kokomo road toward la broquerie to find a drink
snow banked on the shoulders keeps me honest the radio
    cranked high on *born on the bayou*
drifting snow across the windshield erases everything but the
    moment and that's filled with past
winter dreams of sleep hands numb and forgotten the face a
    mask for the dangerous spirit inside

how do you live with snow van gogh's stars roiling in a dark
    blue sky a perfect stillness only cold can bring?
long nights with the moon dazzling in sheets off the fields the
    howl of a far-off dog or coyote
how do you live with snow sane and clear with the nudge of
    love in your heart and the fox long gone?
old henry's dead nothing left but shreds of skin on his
    harmonica and the memory of a song

signature

the movement of his hand across paper was not an
    embellishment but the rehearsal of his name
what he wanted to shape was a motion something of the spirit
    that gave decency its depth

a man practices his signature filling scrap paper with his name
    over and over again
a man enters his signature he repeats the rhythm of his hand
    and the sounding of his name

his name written all over the sheet torn from a scribbler like the
    devotions of a pilgrim
what a man has outside of love is the work he has woven to his
    name the honour of his hand

he sat there at the kitchen table with the wealth of his name
    and the certainty of his god
a man belongs on earth with his children a man works his way
    through his name

kaddish for the old man

your dark eyes and fedora your straight muscled back and your
  long stride
these are gone though I remember everything though I forget
  everything forever amen
it is a poor son who does not hold his father who does not carry
  him toward the next death
I do that it can't be helped but I may not be the vessel you
  hoped to leave behind

I stand on my balcony the beech trees are bare and I don't know
  where you are
perhaps in that grave where we laid you but I am child enough
  to think the sky
what I know will leave with me that evening I saw how empty
  your last room became
I took in the emptiness and circled it the one thing you know
  about me my relentlessness

I start with you standing still in the garden I start with me
  staring from the raspberry canes
I wonder who you are or where because I can see you're not
  there you're lost and I have no father
you're caught between entrances though always one seems an
  exit the other a closed door
there are many moments like this you standing knee-deep in
  west hawk lake or us in the basement before the furnace

but you are my father calling me into the world the world you
  are so afraid of
is this where something goes awry your uncertain call and the
  boy stubborn at the garden's edge

you wake from your reverie and turn toward the back window
    where your love sings
sleeves rolled above your elbows the late sun flashing off your
    glasses how you wanted heaven

and now I'm as old as you ever were or will be as old as I need
    to be to stand for you
I have made my life out of you I am something you didn't know
    blue eyes in the mirror
there's no lightning on the horizon old man no thunder it's a
    quiet rain arriving
earth remembers us for a moment but the garden has gone wild
    and the stone rolls away

small rooms

what matters happens in small rooms a call a letter what comes
   after the intention
the conversation within a man or woman the time taken to find
   the right words
where there is intimacy between thought and word the world
   grows a little still

what matters happens where there's not too much room and
   the walls lean in
the conversation that's possible when the windows freeze over
   with frost on the sill
where there's no one to hear you and change the words the
   world grows a little old

what matters happens where you sit with your elbows on the
   table your feet on the floor
the conversation that rattles through your head all night and
   leaves you worn in the morning
where there are no footprints in the snow and no face at the
   window the world grows forgotten

the man who licked stones

the man in the long coat licked stones memorizing the earth's
    first fire on his tongue
he didn't have time to speak though he had nothing else he
    hadn't come to words
his slow hands hung from the stillness of his torn sleeves
    reaching only to touch what he might remember
with his hands he carefully brushed dust from stones with his
    tongue revealed their rose or cobalt blue
he walked outside town on gravel roads he walked outside love
    too close to worship to say
around him earth's rubble and striations sign and witness of the
    forge he longed to find
his mouth craving volcanoes the taste of ash and rain his mouth
    ground stones in his sleep
I thought he would vanish one day spellbound in his cellar
    among the coal and roots
I thought in the end he might walk into the river with his heavy
    pockets but there was no such privilege for him
with the years I forgot him or he became a shape I couldn't see
    wandering around town
I don't know if he took form again or if it was time for me to
    see but I saw him emerge like a photograph in its bath
he was walking past the church he reeled suddenly with a stiff-
    legged pivot and fell straight on his back
no one falls like that the body in surrender to gravity no one
    falls as if nothing matters and nothing did
his eyes glistening like wet sapphires in snow his dead eyes
    looked through us seeing their way into stone

Earth's Crude Gravities

(2007)

j & a lunch

swivelling on a stool at j & a lunch
a milkshake and hot dog
and you're twelve years old
and you think you're canadian
that version of democracy
james dean and st. laurent
a menno boy with a guttural tongue
and a mission
and you might as well be sitting at some bar
in budapest or prague
turning to look at the danube
or the charles bridge

you're scraggly
a columbine
spare and bare
and you're seeded
where you are buried
but you still dream other places
other tribes and streams
zurich odessa or dniepropetrovsk
or none of them
just the dust of roads
and someone like you
passing through

stealing black cat filters
from rexall drugs
betrayal in your blood
eddie fontaine in your ears
and the evangelist

squeezing the word in his fist
and you think you hear
a waltz dancing through
some sinner's heart
you think you hear
a rhapsody

and it's rock 'n' roll
shaking town and family
it's someone else's pain
you can name
and your limbs loosen
you step out of your shoes
on reimer avenue
looking for john isaacs
and world war two

looking for a story
to get you out
someone else's story
you're choking
on the one you've been given
yet when you turn it over
you find yourself
or someone like you
and rock 'n' roll
is just a revving
of the engine

you swivel to look
out the window
where one of the boys
from friedensfeld
with his duck's ass haircut
is looking for a light

fall (the revelations)

the smell of apples and tomatoes in crates a bonfire in the
   garden burning withered potato plants
mother leaning over the cauldron's steam and father as daylight
   falls raking last vines into the fire

inside the home a bible on the table and linoleum waiting for
   his knees the piano tuned to sabbath
and the child in rapture with jesus with a white horse behold
   the pale horse and seven thunders sounding

the child in wonder at the woman in purple her hands filled
   with abomination and drunk on blasphemy
the beauty of fornication and the trumpets of the city and the
   boy in love with spirit and the bride

dogs whoremongers and the morning star fair and shapely and
   subtle of heart with her solace of love
he steps from the yard the young man lurks near the door of
   words in the dark and black of night

there is so much on earth and in heaven and time at hand for his
   thirst for the sorcery of the world
at home the anxious voice of love calling but he turns toward
   the cinnamon the aloes and the myrrh

I could have remained a worker

the dignity of hands and
something done and seen
lightning through the factory
windows and dreaming
of zorba and water
hired and fired and
rain coming down

my hands at mindless
work and free to be
thinking and finding out
that nothing is absolute
words gods or thought
dreaming of doors
of thunder and all the stairs
and the echo of lost
footsteps at thresholds

tired and used and
spitting angry at money
and rolling wheels and
jesus still knowing
what my hands did
what I could raise and
what I could turn

I could have remained
a worker a broken
honest body I could
have bled red blood
like everything I killed

I could have remained a worker
and the same blood
would have flowed

twice

walking through east vancouver rain the night loose as a slow
    torpedo but with a hard hurt throat
a bell's gong opens doors and it's russians pillaged and sublime
    that liturgy of the seeping wound

asleep the neighbour snores through thin walls of your room
    through even thinner walls of dreams
the heat and motor of him turning over with the thrust of
    pistons and you throwing fish from a truck

you're singing puccini against the wall at least something you've
    heard it feels like rodolfo
your arms spread like a tenor onstage all voice and sluttishness
    an ecstasy a kind of transfiguration

and the smell of fish and water like earth's just been born the
    smell of swamp the creak of oarlocks
and you're there on the water staring at the tentacles of lilies
    and that depth going on beneath them

you don't know death in this fear only relentless birth the
    information going on and on
and you just want to live somehow in this smell and turning
    around you just want to find out

waking to the slap of rain on pavement not sure where you are
    though you know the sound well
you think you were fishing long hours on the shore and
    watching a man in a boat beckoning you

ill at the window and november coming down you reach an
    arm into the weather how easy to be twice
like the funeral you know where a ghost sits on its casket
    waving to invisible relatives as it passes

wind

so the wind riffled the pages
on the pope's coffin
the breath of god a cardinal said
and a day later it ruffled
camilla's hat
her hand reaching up
to hold the feathers in place
and somewhere among mountains
it's turning prayer wheels
and fluttering flags

on the prairies you walk through
god's breath most of your life
if that's how you think of it
and the red tail soars
and long grasses sway
and you're never any further
down the road

a dirt road turns hot
on a still day in july
you may as well sit
and take off your shoes
you may as well find
another god
one without breath
a blue eye
and no stories to spread
among the leaves

leaves stir
just before you feel
the shift of weather
at your wrists
and then a speaking
in your ear
something you know
and nothing more
than clouds muttering
into a rumble and distant
flash and silence
the world waiting
for a spell

and you would raise a prayer
if you had one
you would turn like a wheel
to be human

five nights of rain

rain spatters outside the window inside the world
neighbours watch tv all night you hear explosions through the
    wall
sometimes you miss the madman who lived there with his
    starving cat
you miss his profanity at night and you miss the suicide he
    hoped to commit
and sleepless you listen to *gospodi pomilui* wanting it to bring easter
it's a long night trying to sleep with voices and your body falling
    away

rain drops slowly and heavily on the sidewalk rain with weight
    to it
and you're straying through rooms and snow all you've entered
    and left
nothing stays there's just that motion of your mind unhooked
and you can't hold on no matter earth thin and veiled and
    shivering
you recognize a man glancing away but you lose him in the crowd
you think it might have been him you once waited for

rain dreams the city giddy with its greed and betrayals
you stand beneath an awning seeing with a dead eye
everything collapsing around but you can only take it slow
pavement peels open and funeral doors darken with laughter
a woman stumbles down the street weeping and talking to herself
you can only dread that misery you can only doubt your heart

rain drumming you remember it boiling blue with lightning
where you stood in miles of field defiant and afraid
where you were left with the word and the word failed
there's nothing more to say though something's left to forgive
at dusk through bare trees you see a small light in a house
and in a terminal room a cat curls up on a thin man's lap

rain piddles beneath a street light a raccoon humping across the
    lawn
you've taken a blue torpedo and your blood has slowed to honey
you don't know what needs to be done if anything
a life lost would be something if you knew what it was
a woman shakes out a blanket beneath the back porch light
there's always something like this when the dreaming is done

so many gods

those almost buried in sand
or beneath the sea's surface
those spoken for centuries
others written down for law
those on thrones
and the ones who walk

those who are drunk
those torn by dogs
those who are crazy
and those almost so
those with voice
and those without
those who swat flies
those swatted back

so many gods

the ones who eat
and those eaten
the ones who make love
and those who want to
the ones stillborn
and those in wombs
those who are blind
and those who will be

those on water
and those on dusty paths
those who close the eyes of the dead
and the ones who die
those among the aspen
and those in fields of wheat

so many gods

wise or not
or able to see
what no one sees
they are what they are
the fish in the net
or the net itself

nothing but what's there

1.

lunging up three at a time toward late december light in a small
    window at the top of the stairs
you're goat-footed in a mindless ascent bent forward reaching
    for a world you will enter just like that
at home everywhere in the hymns and garden at home in the
    black book or the deer at clear water
you're holding a japanese orange and staring at the silver tree
    wrapped in angel hair death and song
at home in need like the crow's call and flight that dark
    direction from dawn toward night

2.

you turn pagan one summer a drunkard's tale and a dog the
    horse's harness jangling in the field
your shins blue with bruises you scramble into the poplar's
    rustling where you pray unanswerable prayers
the trellis of dream and memory and you become a killer in the
    trees and a bushful of birds
oh and easter and the town's tongues panting with *seelenangst*
    and a dog's thirst lapping inside your ear
and sin falls away well you swallow it with the questions you
    simply swallow all of it whole

3.

full of yourself on beverley street wearing clothes of eternity
    and singing in a voice that barely sings

always leaning at that window watching maria's brothers on
    their bicycles maria in a dress on the steps
your books piled on the floor as if they can support great
    ceilings your underwood cold and skeletal
upstairs terry plays *don't think twice* on his 12-string and ralph
    laughs dancing alone to gene vincent
richard slathers portraits of jesus with a knife then throws it at
    you because he's too drunk to know the difference

4.

you know nothing all skinny and sure-footing it up the aisle in
    your pride and beatle boy dream
hanging from your necktie like a man of the world when you're
    nothing like that you're walking dna
your bride as lost as you in white and sloe-eyed carrying her
    womb toward the waiting child
you and the woman at each other like honey or resin like
    cockleburs and love like limpet mines
too late one evening eating scallops with butter they look up
    and see each other for once at last

5.

up and down the basement steps your hands at the keys and in
    the kitchen the lord who knows where
well the lord and not the lord that one-hinged door and glory
    that stand-up midnight routine
and always everything in between never bang-on always the
    heel and flaw of ardour work and god

scuffling with that name with every goddamned notion ever a
    dogfight all the way to simple grace
your son and daughter watch you sometimes shaking their
    heads and loving you beyond what you've earned

6.

and you stand on the stairs as if you are already spirit as if you
    are on your way but delayed
like emily's shadow on the landing listening between steps
    stealthy as she turns to climb back up
your hand on the bannister is not for balance but ground the
    grain beneath the polish holding you there
and there means alive grossly gorgeously it means a sharp
    breath that hurts and the smell of want
you meet her at the turn in the stair and you can't say how it
    began but you know that love opens its eyes

7.

descending toward vernazza the ligurian sea and stone steps
    your life suddenly slow and dazzled
a shade in white light against the rocks stepping down with
    your bad knee and the interim of middle age
you're rapt there gazing at an old dream and your body
    remembering it like a first-told fire arriving
wondering if there's a single cell left other than memory's
    provisional contact with that desire
all around you tongues speaking words you don't understand
    but how beautiful the voices how beautiful

stone forgets and lasts

joyce drunk in trieste
through empty piazza ponterosso
slurring down via roma
along via rossini
and the church of sant'antonio
at midnight
his fingers trailing along
the buildings
steadying himself
heading home to nora

stone forgets and lasts
my hands imagine his height
slide along the same stones
but no warmth no prints left
after a hundred years of rain
just someone's memory
something I've read
how they saw his fingers
tracing the walls
finding his way home
broke and pissed
in the twentieth century

the owner of the james joyce bar
sits down with me
worried that I'm drinking rum
and he brings vegetables olives
says I have to eat
joyce he says
would have drunk good wine

from some island
I already forget
but rum he says not rum
and I look down the street
the adriatic a few blocks south
where the fontana baths were
the church of san nicolò
I keep returning to

I can't gather it
the glitter of san nicolò
the candles I light there
for my children
crumbling chimneys
near via punta del forno
lousy american music from somewhere
and rice thrown on a bride and groom
I can't gather
the words and mortar
mopeds buzzing in the thousands
on their way to work
and all the invisible bodies
in high button shoes and bodices
promenading through
the hapsburg years
I can't gather it all

the empire funnelled
through this port
guns silk and books
a late fall storm battering

the battlement of duino
just down the coast
or d'annunzio with his biplane and leaflets
I can't gather all the facts
but they're only touchstones
like a sip of limoncino or
salt fish in some side street restaurant

and I sit there breathing in
all that absence
where joyce pled poverty
and sprawled across a bed
in a single room
writing toward *ulysses*
and nations grinding
into mud and graves
and I can't gather any of it

the silver is polished
again and again
and italo svevo is no one
but bones in the holy field
of the jewish cemetery
and the idea
of leopold bloom
and sailors forever
on the sea always
rowing home

and in our time my love
meets me at the canal grande
we eat grapes from a bag
she calls her son from a pay phone
and we return to the heat
of our room at the alabarda

her fingers touch my lips
and I don't know what they know
though I know they touched
the balustrade at duino yesterday
and I know she knew something there
that was outside of me and her children
and outside of everything else
and my hands are filled with her
and the stones they've brushed
as I feel my way through the lives
of my only history
as long as it takes

thirty birds

naked in twin creek among a slur of fishes
cold water washing me old and human
smooth as a river otter and almost an otter
gazing from eyes I hardly ever fathom

there could be horses drinking at the edge
a grassy slip and splash and skittish long heads
the whites of eyes as I drift by on my back
chest to chest with the cumulus sky

I carry the weight of thirty birds in my heart
well sinner what are you going to do?
I was a perfect hunter town boy weapon
filled with the light of killing and light on my feet

that's long gone in a way though I hear songs
in overgrown gardens or in a mirage of trees
was that when I was becoming a scarecrow
lithe and shabby and threateningly shy?

there's the drowned book and the clouds
god I was thirsty so very thirsty
a horse at the creek all fetlocks and hooves
a nervous animal with peripheral vision

so much bravado beneath the sun
and besotted and dizzy floating downstream
I'm absent if not angelic in the water
or put it another way unknown

still as nothing

you walk quickly always walking when not still as nothing
walking away from your life you walk into it

the field is filled with delicate cries of dying animals
underground families nibble at grain or wait or sleep small hot
    hearts burning

a red-winged blackbird trills
and you belong to it yes sitting at the roadside you belong to it

the other family the one that loves you wants you in the house
for them you are always a silhouette

in early june you broke ice in the ditch with your dark shoe
it was glass cut and sparkling like a chandelier and you breathed

who cannot be still on a bench or alone on a stone
spins among stories uneasy at the pulse

im spiegel

naked from sleep you bend toward the sink
cup your hands with cold water and splash your face
you raise your head and wake into the morning

but in the mirror is someone behind your eyes
beard dripping and eyes bluer than you've ever seen
you stand there in the flesh that is not you

you have not seen your self since the last birth
and you don't wonder after the first shock
you only ask where you've been so long

one face you touch and you reach for the other
you are standing in a room in the world
when the door behind you opens

mockingbird

you remember someone combing
long grey hair in a mirror
and someone laid out in a casket
with a black kerchief on

and someone singing you to sleep
through the milky way
was that last night or today?

which of your burials
will your family attend?

you're as open as the street with its bends and
dead ends somewhere before dawn and maybe
someone like the boy you saw danced
high in a chair on the long arms of men
on his face a child's apprehension and trust
danced into a welcoming whirl the spiral
that appears and vanishes

and play among tall grasses becomes sweat
of brow and muscle and thought just
beginning to know death but forgetting
as the boy is held aloft for moments
only to descend as a man that drunken
man with a mockingbird in his hand

all falls to earth

dinah washington sings
this bitter earth
on the radio

as below
we've known
so above

hauling down
god's blue sail
to hang on the line

no one's well
and the house
is quarantined

the tree comes down
hacked off
at its roots

this bitter earth

all falls to earth
autumn's fruit and
fire

nina simone sings
the last rose of summer
the flaw in her voice

and the old woman
on her last legs
fills the watering can

tsvetaeva

a red horse plods down main street
small puffs of august dust at its hooves
the street bare as starvation
one or two stare then turn away
a horse strains at a light load
the man flicking long reins
as he walks beside a groaning wagon
and its open coffin

a woman with swollen legs
a dead-end rope and all earth
an approaching catastrophe
the animal of her losing its hunger
and her haggard spirit scratching
a grave with a small spoon
and a fierce refusal

a hook in a doorway is enough
or a rafter in a shed
but no they're not enough
nor is a note or a letter
a last conversation is not enough
not even a woman's dead eyes
as she politely shakes a hand
the day before
even this is not enough

columbine

red-winged with
wide-open yellow mouths
they are flying off my balcony
straight for the sun and
I sit there alert and ready
to leap up to catch them
before they fling off
their stems and disappear
into the summer sky

not like the black bird
red-chevroned with a
slash of yellow
spitting out small notes
before its throaty trill
from the roadside marsh
with flies buzzing by and
heat shimmering in the wheat
with a breath of air
in the leaves of the willow
and earth and water and
the old story of angel
finally happy in the wings
of matter

a horse in the apartment

snuffling like an old man clearing his throat
and then again and the clink of iron
a deep sigh and then silence
a thump and an impatient snort
I put down my book and walk to the other room
of course there's a horse in the apartment
it's strange how I keep forgetting
white with dappled hindquarters
this horse has always been around
I used to think one of my grandfather's
but they were brown and black
and I go to the storage room for oats
as it eats I brush and curry its flank
I don't know how far I can go into its eye
though I know its sudden power
what would I do without it?
and yet I so often forget
I put on some russian choral music
and sit back to gaze at this beauty
yes what would I do without it?
the way it sweats and shines in july light
or disappears when it plunges through snowdrifts
it's always been there waiting for me
and I've ridden it sometimes
riding through world and sun
memory goes very deep
the memory I can't even recall
but there's always the problem
of horseshit in the apartment

there's always that beauty

jumping in the asylum
(2011)

crows

those fucking crows those four brilliant gawking crows almost
    shoulder to shoulder on the roof's ridge
that oily sun and the pale cloth of sky slim fingers shaping the
    thin bone of a perfect blue cloud
the crows have wrecked the street with their curses they preen
    in anticipation and are ready

the bushes and trees are silent and reach for a possible suicide
    from the lunging balcony above
and those four crows in their purple soutanes and birettas
    nodding as they wait for someone to emerge
they are patient though they sidle sideways and pause sideways
    and pause finding another view

the work of crows is sometimes the work of murder but always
    the work of witness and last rites
the cloud has charred and begun to crumble falling in flakes in
    soot and ashes all over the world
the crows hunch beneath the ash growing grey and annoyed as
    they endure a death that no one sees

daughter

bareheaded with the dark hair of a thousand years of fields and
    infidels the lanterns moon and silhouette
who clothed her in the naked summer who placed her in the
    garden grown from ancient seeds?

barefoot in a pale blue dress brown eyes squinting as she whirls
    in surprise to see who calls
on the anvil of july hollyhocks and the dark inside of the tin
    shed the oily grass smell of the mower

stunned for a moment in the back yard slowed by the syrup of
    humid air and sun and the rasp of bees
she bends at the waist and moves to begin her gaze away and
    her long arms spread exquisite

she tilts between beck and flow sowing a voice and everything
    turns and turns again and everything goes on
juice drooling from fallen plums bark peeling from the birch
    and the sky blanched to apocalypse

who calls her among the tools the rakes and hoes who calls her
    through her feet to her hair?
who calls calling a slender stream of fish of rivers, and rushes
    calling from the dark arch of the bridge?

still life without einstein

can't do it can't hold an apple in the light can't look at it long
    enough to become no time at all
or limes in the spanish bowl green thunder rolling low through
    quaking aspen and balsam poplar

can't think that green not the green that moves and won't be
    still the green that green doesn't know
carve your thumbnail into orange peel and the scent
    overwhelms colour and abandons shape

can't hold up the sky there is no structure for that but the blue
    curve that comes to light as thought
the arc of the mind's traffic hands and knees toward what can't
    be reached passing what's left behind

and in the window who is that washing the woman's feet his
    face in shade but not his long hands
he leans into light to kiss her feet but einstein has left and no
    one paints still life anymore

son

you were dancing in some rural wedding hall your daughter on
    your feet her small hands holding on
how do you account for seething pinpoints of worlds in the
    night sky and you moving in a drunken rhythm?

sick with smoke and finding your way to the unlit motel you
    found your way to your lost wife
your son waiting for you beyond the flesh big-eyed smiling and
    turning his face toward you

reaching for a milky sea summoning the sailor from his ghost
    ship where he stood ancient watch
overboard on high seas a swimmer swimming canals and straits
    swimming for a harbour of sun

the boy found then in his muscular rush through reeds and
    fables spun in a circle and breaking in
half-dead in his bulky arrival purple cord around his throat and
    blood coursing through the delta

alexandria seville or winnipeg all flowing rivers of passage and
    light in those narrow streets
accidents of encounter of human wish and ambition blind want
    and sorrow and what's remembered

and the man born a child one of the unchosen blown astray by
    storm squall or blue prairie wind
born a son into mothering and fathering born into his own
    loneliness within the lonely tale

jumping in the asylum

are you ravaged fire licking along your arms?
you have memorized photographs words and hands
what flinches at the corner of your eye are you raptured?
remember nijinsky how he stood in the asylum
black shoes and suit remember how he leapt suddenly up
heels together his shadow haunting the wall behind him

that lift and why? miles of neuron and synapse a chemistry
and remember the ghost of a rose and splendour but why?
in the hall in the miles of hall and walls and the current
pulsing cellular through the young man gone
gone with his secret smile gone into the rooms and halls
into the old man who leaped for himself and the other yes

why and when there is no why are you raptured?
arms flayed are you ravished? milk brother to jeanne
d'arc losing all for the voice listening defiant and mute
the old man hanging there his hands fluttering beside him
what wasn't called but spoke from tendon and ligament
sparking the mind all metacarpal and phalange

are you seared in the conflagration are you?
hooved yellow-eyed and slender with hunger
it paces before the window yammering in the dark
nerves of words and the clicking of bones picked clean
throats of birds and early light among the leaves
high in the trees there where it begins are you ravaged?

a child's face and a memory of first obliteration
awe and breaking the lost bride of that shadow
his hands small quick souls on their way to death
do you whistle where you loiter are you raptured?
the current through him through all the grey scaffolding
a torrid nonchalance of rufous pistil and stamen

the hall is empty a cleaner sweeping dust and shade
do you smell perfume in wisps do you know?
a person is not a person in the marathon of sperm and eggs
who is light enough to separate who is chaff?
culled from the bone fire raked and combed to grass
there must be a way to leave the earth behind

dragging the river

combing the bottom of the dark river for a disappearance a
    wrinkle on water and then an absence
the raking of water of the unseen and hauling up the detritus
    of town wheels ropes and rust

dragging the river for the child lost abruptly in the river's door
    and in the heat of a july afternoon
could there be such vast want to be water to rock in that light
    where it bends and turns gold?

whose hand in the water whose handkerchief and slow grief
    whose flip-flops covered with sand?
did anyone see footprints filled with child did someone reach
    and touch a warm shoulder turning?

horses plod along the bank raising dust and sweat they haul the
    invisible load and voices call
calling for the bride in her black dress beneath the poplars or
    walking away from the willows

raking through water fish and reeds raking for a body rolling it
    over and over until it's hooked
tines tearing through clothes and grasping time rolling forward
    into the past and rolling on

moon reaches into water and tempts us but does not reach deep
    enough voices growing away
I had a boy she says I had a son and for a moment that is all for
    a moment she lives with that

gone like the bell-ringer's wife

gone like the bell-ringer's wife like the voice in the garden gone
    like the good ships and fair winds
how long since you've tasted your shadow licking it where it
    lingers on the white stucco wall?
and how long gone the story of old days your mother told
    before bedtime the story of the drowned sailor?

the storm was rolling in and gods were weeping did we hear
    that sound the gods were leaving earth
did we hear the door close the blue door at the top of the steps
    did we hear our rude words to strangers?
we turned from them the wind riding through the orchard
    shaking drunken fruit to the ground

sometimes we thought we heard them talking faintly as if
    through a veil words at the root of us
sometimes we ran across paths that were still warm animal or
    god it was always hard to tell
and when the world went silent for a while we asked the band
    to strike up we learned not to whisper

everything sank beneath the sea the silver spears and buckles
    the basins and the banquet bowls
islands swamped one by one the islands disappeared leaving
    nothing but summer and flotsam behind
and people prayed with thick tongues they worshipped like
    cattle bawling in the noonday heat

did we see her lying beneath the wreckage of her dress on her
     elbows and arching her back?
always there was night at the stream's mouth and a way
     through night seed dropping into the rift
the bell tolled three times the rope uneasy as the bell-ringer
     dragged his feet toward the empty house

o'keefe bones

a place where you never heard thunder not thunder not the
   sound that reaches into you for a moment and leaves
leaving nothing behind to hold you nothing to terrify leaving
   nothing but the rubble of a fallen city
it's a place you can't return to there is too much going on the
   only church you love to enter is the empty one
sitting at the back always near the door and no one in sight you
   listen for the sound that was left behind

awake in the pew rafters and hymns and stained glass the
   stations of the cross around all that want
and you sully the emptiness with your body the smell of worry
   of world the smell of your birth
alive you sit there in your memory and memory before that
   knowing everything always leaves
you sit there and don't belong to what you see or know you
   belong to nothing but what you hear

and what you hear is what you heard or what you think you
   heard echo fade and doppler effect
what you don't hear anymore is the word any word you don't
   hear solace and there is no astonishment
what you hear is the wind in march or perhaps july or that
   exhalation you think you hear at night
human ruin the serenity of the building fallen what is there is
   the sun on o'keefe bones beside a white wall

goya's room

where he sat beneath a dark window a dog caught in its
    festering life
beyond baying or the moon or anything like that just gazing at
    the brazen night and
a long year of deaths and empty rooms and mouths open with
    sentences
things said he remembers vaguely the drift or perhaps a precise
    phrase

with no word that works only that it is unsaid only that it
    happens only that things
disappear and for him that is forever legs slipping deeper in muck

he has not wasted enough time he thinks he has not listened to
    enough music
not taken in enough winter light or strings of pearls he has not
    stopped counting the days

thinking he has done too much of death's work that usefulness
    to the machine
shifting gears or pumping the brakes one year wrapping
    windows to be shipped
in heaven they said there was not even the dignity of dying but
    a small spittle of greed

on thursday night he dreams of water the splash of a kingfisher
    his lover's eyes
how they suddenly glisten with a quicksilver of tenderness
dreaming on the weekend of a silken gown the red of no flowers
but the red of a certain blood perhaps

understanding he has not done enough of death's work that
    uselessness
that drenched black suit he can't take off his fingers locked in
    the gloves
crossed on his chest that delight of undoing what he has not
    done doing nothing
on his back the bartender staring up at the lit jewels of bottles
    behind him
remembering every brilliant face and bracelet every carpenter
    with a black thumb
and every story-teller with a stutter that he watered

so it goes in his room with shutters battened against the smell
    of damp
earthy night the heat of fire in the river sliding through him and
the old dancer with serpent arms with a famous story on her hips
and the desire of her flaring nostrils he applauds what he saw
in the eye of the stage and what he can't hold

he throws himself at walls scorched walls one winter night
    throwing himself
into the depth of a man only a man one mind's man and the fire
    guttering out

he works there in the room blowing on the embers and
    arranging himself into disarray

loose in the house of fundamentalism

you go dancing around your room banging off red walls
    pictures swinging wildly on their hooks
shivers down your backbone tailfeathers ruffling and you
    playing piano with a ball-peen hammer

words and doors unhinged as night blooms in the brain's soil
    flowering like the watered grave
you're flagrant and lost sniffing for primal heat kicking your
    way through the room's furniture

nighthawk or crow this is the word loose in the house of
    fundamentalism wings beating against glass
cries of blue fire anger's call for vengeance rocking on your toes
    knocking the clock from the wall

a quiver in your bones old as old but who's counting bog
    piltdown man and lucy in the sky
bestial and defrocked some god undone with one blue eye lazy
    and the other dark and crazy

you skid scuffing linoleum all feathers and mischief careless
    damage along the million-mile wall
bitching at some yellow-eyed parrot *not enough* nothing
    memorized just holy ghost and a slippery foot

wella wella sings the crow *bird is the word* hopping from leg to leg
    a cockeyed killer and awry
wella wella next flight out of here heading anywhere and
    anything goes and always it does

a dark boat
(2012)

a dark boat

you are alone
and you mean precisely that

half-lit by the lamp
you have nothing

on the wall a poster
of a fadista you once heard

long-legged in her longing
waitress in a three-table café

so far to go from
a nursing mother to death

the world is quiet outside
though you know it's writhing

you can't speak
about the world

the fadista sang
of a dark boat

you make do
with the night you have

the clarinet's brilliant dream

saints and mary gliding
through narrow streets
a dark-haired boy
slowly marching
behind the band
his eyes wide and
shining

sobbing when
the band disperses
the night coming down
and his mother's hand
calming him into
the clarinet's brilliant
dream

marching around
the church
down a roman road
marching through
grass and flowers and
beneath the sparrow's
wings

marching with
light feet and
blowing eerie
sounds through
the broken branch
in his little
hands

and the clarinet
dreams the boy
on the road no
one has walked
dreams him toward
the band's silver
encore

blind in the summoner's arms

he stumbled down the stairs
into the garden of eyes

leaving the stone wall's shade
he slid through a fence and came upon the cedar

a dream of hanging ladders of fire
and fearing the wordless night ahead

he lay down in darkness
blind in the summoner's arms

the garden filled with swollen leaves
of tongues of words

a long unknown night
and no one there but him

leaving his shoes behind
barefoot as an orphan

lorca

heard water in the aqueduct
before dawn in la colonia

and if there had been light
could have seen childhood

water flowing is the shortest time
eternity is a poor word for this

what can be done about a dream
of black veils and a crucifix

what can be done when you've
forgotten your mother's prayer

only death listens to fear
only his body hangs on to him

smelling the road's dust
hearing the rifle's bolt

dark night of the tree

the tree
where john lay drunk
with christ the swoon
of that of that love
drunk and yes drunk
among the paths of
a spanish garden

yellow eyes staring feral
from the top of
the stone wall and
a ladder into
night's turret

bare feet damp
with dew the
cedar's scent the
only way toward
what toward what
was john's abysmal
ridiculous
bliss

forgetting himself
and skinned but
the wind but
the cedar leaning
over them
how can you
forget so far how
can you?

only the tree
remains and a few
words lost among
languages the tree
broken
to a man's height
and want

you stand
there in spanish
sun before the tree
a dazed man
in a stupid time
that moment betrayed
again and you
still wanting the
darkness that burns
in the soil of
soil

and wouldn't you
love to wouldn't
you breathe
in the old branches
of the cedar
bellowing like tom waits
in november
calling like flint
for a fire
wouldn't you love

that disease

green dress

it will kill me
kill me

you in bare feet and a green summer dress

there's a long car
around the corner
perhaps a limousine
or a blue cadillac

you in the pale light of your summer dress
so light it flutters when the air stills

your eyes closed
your head with its black hair
tilted back to the sun

it will kill me
whatever it is
this will kill me
what I've carried forever

I don't like long cars
they hold a human
like a little seed
while the driver never talks
there's just too much distance

but you across the yard
naked in your green dress
you

sol y sombra

the cool noonday moon
rivets a bare landscape

magdalena of the garden
playing to the light

but her voice calling
from the shade

a line of light slides
along the shine of a street

filtering through the lattice
of a lace house

from a white balcony above
a parrot's blue come-on

while estrella dries her black hair
in the sun

barrio santa cruz

sauntering toward her marriage
in the old jewish quarter alone
and bare-shouldered she
moves through centuries of
perished footsteps and ash

moors and jews soleares
from triana drifting across
the river and the barefoot
walk of faith a band
gathering in some street

processions come and go
hooded men staggering beneath
the masks of history
while she carries the dark
accounts

light from a side street
draws her around a bend
toward the street of the fallen
where her marriage waits
in the arms of a thief

palmas

an echo through
olive groves brown hills
scattered with poppies

how the world began with
a sharp handclap then
staccato fingers swirling

across strings like
a devil fleeing
through sacromonte

melisma soleares and
the white-sailed ships
drifting home empty

the rhythm the rhythm
is there in the skeletal trees and
hands

handclaps becoming the dark
hands of the gardener
at day's end

a short history of
crazy bone

(2015)

I

crazy bone is born
at the river

each time she meets it
and goes under

it takes a moment
that passes away

she lands a fish
with bare hands

crazy bone knows
where the still pools lie

nothing still that I know
but what do I know?

31

as she rises for the day
she leaves her smell in the grass

I was known once
that's for sure

the grass slowly
releasing her shape

but what remains
of the lowly and the high?

all that mating
to feed the earth

crazy disappears and appears
through thin drifts of mist

that endless
hunger

god eat
god

34

crazy tugs a red dress from the line
behind the abandoned house

I will wear this wedding
and I will marry

she lets her blue dress slide
to pool around her feet

naked in the sun
and dazed

I will marry nobody
and no one marry me

crazy picks wild flowers
to weave a headdress

with this crown
I marry myself

she slithers
into the red dress

ah look at me
in my wedding colours

I am thief
of the rainbow

I am anything
I was born to

arms raised
crazy dances like a flame

making
my escape

me myself
and I

35

crazy remembers
and recites the names of gods

loki christ
and whatever

moloch greed
adonai and before

she sits down
on a bale of hay

scratching her arm
till it bleeds

the ones with the heads
of birds

crazy punctures a tick
with her thumbnail

grandmothers and
the grandfathers

and me sitting here
like an old crow

36

a thin night
and long

the owl is near
and small bones everywhere

long time
no see

crazy listening
to cries

a still cedar
in slender light

new moon is nothing
but a tease

lighting up
the slaughter

like a wing a breeze
strokes her neck

crazy on her elbow
propped against a tree

it's just like this
how love arrives

that great old
come on

swinging the door
wide open

long time
no see

46

crazy bone balances on her toes
reaching for a plum

what the rain offers
and the heat fattens

cupping it in her hand
she licks off the dust

it glows royal purple
as she holds it high

something
will die

for this to become
spirit

juice drools
from her mouth

crazy spits the stone
and wipes her lips

it's a honeymoon
and me near drunk

50

the river has a mouth
and I have ears

crazy bone draws her shawl
around her shoulders

she stands by the water
of approaching winter

a broken willow
dipping into the narrow seine

she's found an icy moon
in the later afternoon

it is pleasing to me
the end as the beginning

one hand filled
with stones

crazy calls across the river
her other hand rising to her mouth

58

birch are almost invisible
against the fields of snow

bird tracks littered
around a mulberry

this is the white page
the old ones said

this is where
we learn to read

and where language
melts away

crazy on her knees
makes prints with her hands

like grauman's
I should be in movies

me and
meryl streep

I was thinking
of something like freedom

jack rabbits owls
and blood

she sweeps snow from a broken chair
with her bare hand

she balances on its three legs
by leaning forward

her hand
to her chin

like the thinker you'd think
rodin in a trance

but nothing left
to think

62

at night
the ghosts of geese

white-bellied
and flying low

me pale
as a gibbous moon

thinking clear and
not thinking at all

the smell of me
is the smell of god

and then nothing
in the sky

not even the sound
of wings

63

yesterday I was a sparrow
falling to earth

today I am
a miró tadpole

crazy takes off her shoes
and hangs them around her neck

she walks into the stream
holding her skirt to her waist

her shawl slides into the water
and the current takes it

like an irish maiden
with seaweed clinging to my thighs

and all the milleniums
just pass away

like slippery silver fish
gliding by my ankles

66

crazy reaches the end
of a path

she stops to gaze
across a clearing

the shadows of trees
grow longer

standing here
like the god of all time

and maybe not
quite that

servant of thunder
slave of this place

something
high and mighty

me and the gods
nose to nose

and who can say
whatever

an owl with
a bone to pick

a blackbird
with its grievous wound

76

one foot jiggling
I was listening to the radio

listening to drunken notes
from a piano

that growly voice
with his hammered klavier

remembering a parade
in seville

with its crosses
and christ held high

remembering a brilliant
snow-lit night

and further back
where the seasons run together

my grandparents
ten thousand years ago

them walking across
the world

always moving always
on their way to water

and water always
on its way

78

well if it isn't the end of me
and harvest around the corner

that fat orange moon rolling
toward me like a cannon ball

tomorrow the scythe
and everything laid out golden

crazy pulls out her bottle
and salutes the moon

in the dark I wonder
who I am

in the light
I wonder the same thing

but it's all a stupid
wonder

spirit inside spirit
inside spirit

I knew a drunkard once
who blessed me

80

how do I know god
when I don't believe?

well I don't know god
anymore than god knows me

and that's backwards
like some lennon song

backwards like
reading mirrors

but I know of thee
ah yes with red wings in the marsh

I know of thee
and ambrosia

and maybe the secret
is in the dance

you know whirling about
until you think you're seeing things

that eye
inside the eye

ha that would be
me

or someone
probably someone

85

mirror my mother said
look in the mirror and comb your hair

on her knees
crazy gazes into the river

listen I can whistle mozart
something churchy

or plunk piano keys
like schubert in that hotel bar

window mirror
on the wall

and those bulls those hidden
unbelievable bulls

crazy splashes her face
then stands up slowly

I am becoming old
becoming something or other

funny how old is always ahead
even though it's been

passing through the gateway
with its hunger

but sometimes
there's no going further

the gate groping
on its hinge

86

crazy makes a fist
then unfolds it

look at my monkey hands
all the lines and wrinkles

a lot of memory
a lot of

she looks at her hands
turning them over

and here she taps her head
there are free thoughts

crazy watches light grow dim
and night moving in

there's no cockatoo on my shoulder
though there might as well be

she gathers a few sticks
for a fire

there are thoughts crazy
with colour and shape

crazy turns to hear coyotes
wailing in the distance

ah they're hungry
or are they free?

94

I remember and
so I am

the afternoon
I almost drowned

the taste of
sunlit water

which I wouldn't remember
would I if I'd died

all the lies
and maybes

and there are lies
that hold fire

cold facts
I don't recall

she gestures dismissively
with her hand

who isn't in a story
now and then?

102

I heard a child
singing all night

arriving and fading
with the wind

but yet I do not know
my own breath

I know only
the owl

and its
plunder

the horse
unbridled

I know the trout
and the river

and beneath
the sun

the days of grass
swaying

and the child singing
among the leaves

songen

(2018)

babbling, that's what it came to

babbling, that's what it came to, rising
to speechlessness, that ladder of desire,
how many times you've been there, top
of the tower, and how many times you've
fallen, the sorry old story, boring and a
lie, there was no tower, but there was
a ladder, lying beneath an oak, ancient
with broken rungs, and bones littererd
at the edge of a clearing, and you sitting
in tall grass, watchful for predators,
your body atremble with beginnings, and
a worm at your words, you were babbling
to your first love, with sounds no other
had ever heard, sounds that were lost
eventually within the landscape, your voice
growing into landscape

100,000 miles

wind talking across long grasses and water,
riffing along earth's surfaces, where it goes,
what destination, what stone in your shoe,
what roadkill, what crows lurching slowly
above fields of wheat, what killdeer dragging
its wing in circles, and from an abandoned
pontiac what late night music, what still
cold nights in december, what soggy ditches
and reeds, what cans and bottles and hubcaps,
what dead cigarettes, lipstick tubes, from
the dark distance what animal cries, and
what shabby shoes in the 100,000 miles
of your brain.

winter blindness

it's been so long, that voice I heard down
the hall, waking me abrupt, not a family
voice, but familiar, arguing, it seemed, with
my father, and raising me from the dream
of drowning, but that was long ago, I was
still becoming human and my wounds were
ears, who was the egg man from whom I came?
held to the light, candled and found flawed,
leaving my room then, and moving along
the moonlit hall, wrapped in the voice I never
saw, a kind of winter blindness.

landscape, a child's mind

landscape, a child's mind, it is everything,
aules, a grave too big, make one place
everywhere, and the child lives there, loose
as the wind, though he be no star, but a
mortal fire, quick-eyed he sees motion
in the stillness, a heartbeat in a stone,
instinct in camouflage, and everywhere,
right here, moves his mind, from root to
blossom, sliding on the blade of the gardener's
shears.

fold up the maps

my friend, fold up the maps, directions are shutting down,
the believing man walks through the square with his hammer,
he's looking for a tree, he's looking for some nails, my friend,
expect the silence that falls when laughter dies, well, expect
nothing, but wait, and the waiting will be long, wait for
something almost forgotten, a distant howl, that's what it is,
a dogged howl, a coyote's yip and yowl which holds laughter,
which holds sorrow, like a train's whistle passing through
the prairie night, that was a sound, I used to call it freedom,
now we must bury the maps, but remember where they're
laid, this is not time for journeys, but that time will come.

this room, my aldgate

this room, my aldgate, looks out over a path, gulls
on the roof cry in their kerfuffles, all that family
disorder, the young ones leaping at the edge, but
backing off with much fluttering of wings, a child
wails in its stroller, wanting what we all want,
a bicyclist sings loudly as he pedals past, music
leaking from his earbuds, how happy and out of
tune a human can be, goya's dog trotting behind
a tottering dowager, all heels and bouffant, with
tears in her eyes, and an old-world man, brown-
backed in sandals, turns, listening for a moment
to the distant cries, the dog gazing at the sky.

glossolalia at the star club

die grosze freiheit, the naked street where everything
passes, where there are no souvenirs, but clowns cons
and evangelists dealing in mockery and farce, and the
band on adrenaline bailing out of time, trying to locate
little richard hammering triplets like esquerita with his
pompadour, no need but the full breath of release, and
the singer testifying in tongues, sliding along the edge
of the demonic, and tearing his shirt like a man possessed
by jubilation, shredding words with slippery menace, a
pentecost of a god dancing like lava from earth's furnace,
and spilling over the horizon and, sister rosetta, didn't
the boy find peril in the ecstatic?

scenes, 1968

scenes, 1968, bulgarian days, snejana's dark
elegance, and me sun-stroked into a whorl
of time and sound with nothing to weigh or
decide, barnett's mandolin melodious upstairs,
him singing *I'll be coming round the mountain*,
and mel warming ancient coffee, then shredding
drum tobacco into a zig-zag paper, scenes like
flickering super-8 films, and books in piles,
nine-deep, or scattered across the floor, records
spinning, climbing bass, guitar driving *shakin'*
all over, and ralph marrying his beloved,
richard dancing euphorically, alone, wheeling
round and round, then seizing a large ash tray,
once more around, like a discus thrower, and
flinging it through the window with a cry, all of us
on our knees, outside at 3 a.m., wasted and puttying
a new pane of glass.

syngen, he was

syngen, he was, o'connell leaping from the bath,
and dauncen naked in the kitchen, to work out
his first poem, and the last, at the table, among
the crumbs and stains, this happens once only,
him finding a sound, his sounding, a pool of water
at his feet, singen like a frog all night, a bearing
for the lost, for himself, in his wiles, his song
of divine murder, the beggar's bruise, he did sing
it, in winnipeg, gruff in his throat, afraid and
thirsty, infinity closing in, running fingers through
his bristling hair, I can sleep, he said, and he slept.

rejoicing, the folye

we were songen and rejoicing, well, singing anyway,
goodly poison in our veins, flopping fish, as it were,
sermon on the mount, tanked and weathered, witless
to the dregs, our folye, our only haberdashery ruined,
and us pissed and singing, enough already, enough say
the wise, but never enough, breathless is soon enough,
and always a child waiting, hauch and whiff, another
breath, and the perfume of earth, and we were songen,
you know, because we were dying, we were dying
and rejoicing in our pagan hymns.

listen, the man says he wasn't crazy enough

listen, the man says he wasn't crazy enough, there's
only one time around, so get unhinged, and he got loose
enough to get away, loose enough to say no because
it was yes, loose enough to find a few words, to find
a little music in his skull, but not nearly unhinged enough,
not crazy enough, too wary, not trusting the gods, not
losing his life enough and holding on to what flotsam
there was, floundering in the trash of foundering ships,
calling out yes and meaning no, listen, completely
unfit and shouting some kind of shrapnel, land ho,
or some expletive, getting loose, learning how to live
without worship.

thinking, like kaspar hauser playing piano

thinking, like kaspar hauser playing piano,
those opaque melodies, or something like,
pried from beneath black keys, and smudged
onto white ones, notes falling between, notes
out of time, him banging the strings with a
hammer, wrong, eh? and bending time into
words, sibylline, or maybe not, it's all delphic
anyway, them lurking behind unlit scrims,
and thinking the new moon will cool his cranium,
it always does.

a dream metaphysical

a child, that's what I felt like, in a conversation
with traherne in his study, talking about school,
thrashings and nostalgia, the bible's shortest
verse, he thought, was jesus' reaction to the
child chimney sweep, and ian dunn arrived
for a drink, seemed to know thomas well,
sometimes staying at the manse, quaffing
while thomas talked about angels, and
then dunn turning things on their heads,
sin as salvation, for instance, and sobriety
as the root of idiocy, and thomas laughing,
slapping the reading desk with his hand
until the skull jumped, and him saying
he'd like to be buried right there, beneath
the desk, but first he'd like a drink, but ian
was reciting marvell, and suddenly he was
gone, with the skull under his arm, and I
left as well, falling from the sky.

walking, the moon lit high

walking, the moon lit high, through a graveyard,
afeard of mystery, of ghost candles wavering
above graves, the dead rising to their feet,
fluttering like silk, and me on the stage of mein
grauf, empty, and open as a gorge of hunger, open
to the moon's grinning skull, walking through
my curtain call, hands flappin, and me bowing,
and turning around in this misdirection, in this
disintegration, calling for the famliar ones, but
they are no longer familiar, they are whispering
with their new familiars, the gossip of the dead.

putrefaction

putrefaction, yes, it's often on my mind,
not oftener than it was, but with a smell
to it now, the harbour at low tide, the
scent of a rose bush in the backyard,
and I see it in the flamenco dancer's
articulate articulated hands, raised
above her head, finding the spotlight,
that is perhaps the deeper beauty now,
not that things are becoming something
else, but that the hands are already appalling,
and exquisite, one holds one's breath, as
they say, each time beholding for the first
time what has been beheld forever,
remembering how my young daughter,
watching a ballet, believed she was all
dancers, and she was.

wrong, he said

wrong, he said, wrong wrong wrong,
and he was right, this was no bach
cantata, I was singen like a drunken
gull, stealing notes from something
I might have heard once, and we was
sitting in the man's car, for the ride
he had offered, and me laughing
at a joke I remembered, but he just
looked sad and said the lord be with
you, and she was, the wind at the open
window, I know she was.

spider

spider, hurtling across the floor, a dark blur caught
at the corner of an eye, a moving stigma, a poet's
favorite beast, he sees the fears around it, the weight
of stories it carries, but the poet grows ordinary in
his words, forgetting that the wise never claim wisdom,
just like the spider doesn't name itself, but moves
invisibly around the room, until it decides to make
a run for it, a spurt across a blonde hardwood floor,
and then it is named.

mri

slick as a trombone, sliding into the casket,
a small intake of breath, *breathe* the voice says,
miles davis cupping his trumpet with a mute,
a slippery sound, almost an escape, a caesura,
hold, hold what? my breath, yes, but the watery
applause in some club as well, bill evans having
drifted away from his solo, and my hands open,
a kind of love, it's what you feel, and your eyes
open to the casket's lid, and you are sealed in,
but miles is playing, and max roach has a perfect
touch on the ride, *relax*, like a dead man reading
the inside of his eyelids, just like a memory.

the sperrit moves

a bird twittering on a branch, a wren,
a sparrow, the one with a forked tail,
mother listening as always, with intent,
alone from us even as her want brims,
as she kneels to pray serious words in
the silence of her room, the words guiding
her somehow through a house of misery,
the demented cradling dolls and humming
lullabies, and as she disappears, day by
day, into some other land, she sits beside
one who has long left, lolling in her chair,
two solitudes and a solidarity, and she
picks up a fallen doll to return to its ancient
mother when its eyes click open, long-lashed
with a stare, meeting mother's blue eyes,
and the sperrit moves between them,
come dark sister with your salves and
mercy.

flautrijch

flautrijch, he says, meaning his heart,
some kind of finch on its perch beside
an open door, agitated and ruffling
its wings, waiting for the right moment,
you don't simply leave, everything
has its time, but you must be ready,
and he is, he thinks, the yellow bird
cocking its head, and his heart fluttering
a little more every day, *flautrijch* like
a flame in a cave.

einsehen

einsehen, said rilke, looking for something
not him, the pacing panther, for instance,
looking into the raw heart, the weight of
its burden, and looking back at himself
through green eyes, *einsehen*, how to see
yourself, not from a mirror or photograph,
seeing the lost wilderness in your eyes
from the wild other, the centuries of surrender,
the brutality of that, your heart a sleek thing
now, polished to politesse and romance,
the animal caught in its survival.

ein leiermaun

a moment, rising from a chair, a sudden
crimp in my side, and I speak, saying *friesen*
you're old, and I don't know who I am, or
rather, I know who it is I am speaking to,
there is such a distance between the two
of us, and I'm wondering who this friesen is,
and what my name might be, fraudulent,
ein leiermaun, dogged by the sun, playing
a song which is not his, nor anyone else's,
come to think of it, just getting to myself.

even her shadow

even her shadow, as she moves past the windows,
is beautiful, moonlight melting through the blinds like
sunflower oil, a silhouette on its way to the bathroom,
the smell of night in the room, and me about to fall back
on my pillow, falling into sleep, but hanging on, eyes heavy-
lidded, wanting to see her shadow return, its contour,
its silent motion, unsure-footed across the rug, then leaning
into bed, drawing the duvet about her, like a child, until
only her small face shows, a sigh, and she's gone, out
of this room, this home, away, and I touch her hair.

dying to be seen

looking, like herzog, into the eye of predation,
all that rapacity and fecundity, looking into
the mirror, getting rid of a cowlick, and the
child says to the man, I am not really here,
I ended when I began, there's just this face,
a face I think I've seen somewhere before,
and the man replies, without thinking, ah well,
a tumbler and a juggler be, slippin and slidin
like that scorched acrobat, dauncen through
like a wild man at midnight, the street ablaze,
and the ghost, dying to be seen, is standing
on the corner, where a drummer bangs on an
upturned bucket, and there he is, little richard,
with his eyeliner, all lit up on a flatbed trailer,
syngen *wop-bom-a-loo-mop*, ah ghost, welcome
to this great house.

a man asleep in the terminal

on his side, his knees drawn fetal,
and his hands, palms together,
between his thighs, his shoes on
the floor, tipped over beside him,
socks rumpled around his ankles,
he could get up, but his shoes have
grown too large, he could get up,
and walk away with baby steps,
but he has not yet been born.

new work

lingering

no one gets through the gates of canterbury, they're
all in public houses, in some town along the way,
or on the road, but no one arrives, there have been
closed doors, and thresholds where you leaned, gazing
out or looking in, a caesura that leaves words dangling
on either side, as if that hesitation stays still forever,
a home for ambiguity, a place to hold longing, but
a bell rings in the city, a call for certainty, a doorway
in which you can't linger, catching the shade, and
you lose the moment, once again, walking loose
and into the weather.

pterodactyl

pterodactyl glides across the water with leathery wings,
long legs lowering as it nears the shore, and I'm waking,
confused, coming awake to being human, the species,
how does it work, this sapiens, this brain? these hands,
trembling slightly with age, the body, what is meant by
this blessed body? confused by the species, where are
the border lines? between salmon and sapiens, hawk and
human, the heron standing still in the shallows, priested,
yes, then snaky as it uncoils, then stalking on stick legs
into prehistory, looking for momentary flashes of light
just beneath the surface, stabbing swiftly into the shimmer
of a fish, a brief life, and it begins to come back to me,
the necessary earth, it comes back, my tongue-tied
non-existence, the heron rising, legs dangling for a moment,
a gaunt ghost of extinction, a million years of it, and me,
word-spawned bait.

imagine that

lightning sizzled, slanting down like the hidden
sun's sperm, like refracted light, but there I've
gone too far, the language won't do, as if there
are gods and goddesses on the move, in the air,
among the trees, and me a secular man longing
for mesolithic mind, something undivided, like
a stone eye, the man thirty thousand years old,
standing inside a fall of rain, and though that was
yesterday it's as far as I can go, dreaming back
on my own ghost path, hearing that voice across
the water, and caught there, for a moment, on
the river's bank, earthbound as a dodo bird,
yes, a dodo bird, imagine that.

monkey hands

a distant grumble of thunder, the kind that
arrives slowly, and the child slipping out of
the bedroom window, a boy in peril, standing
inert in the ozone smell of the approaching storm

a boy holding the fear of beasts, of owls and
demons, his eyes never having been lost in
such darkness before, trying to be still, deepening
his breath

a far-off flash inside a cloud, boiling in the night
sky for a moment, seraphic, the boy hearing
his blood, like thunder from another time

he raises his hands to his face, they're monkey
hands, he can see that, him knowing suddenly
the darkness inside, what he is, the earth of
himself, his skin a thin border

and he's boy and chimp, he's an unborn thing
always being born, and there's a noise in the
hedge, something alive, the boy grabbing a
low branch and climbing a tree, hugging the
trunk high up, that home where there are no
stories to make him human.

valentine's day itch

guttural cawing from the crow-littered roof,
them dropping clam shells and me tossing
chunks of baguette, they glide down and
half a dozen become two dozen in seconds,
waddling around me, is that love? their bright
eyes on this host, as they've been on all
the ghosts of us, walking pale along streets
we've built, language and coins and desire,
all that detritus of the made world and
that itch, that valentine's day itch to keep
the species going, though by now we've
replaced it with chocolates and roses and we
blame it on malory and the knights of the
round table, that ancient romance, always
some holy grail in the rear-view mirror, and
them clam shells clattering on the roof.

smooth-hulled gull

a smooth gull, a smooth-hulled gull,
rowing through the air with graceful oars,
crying like nostalgia, circling higher and
higher, and the cry becoming necessary
in its distance, a cry of memory, an orientation
of prayer, the way it becomes slippery and
promises hope like the rainbow, evanescent
arches of flight building the most ancient skyways,
where spirits have crossed into unmapped
lands, and then in a moment it dismantles all
the scaffolding of heaven, swooping low, and
splashing to a halt, almost a fish.

ghost seed

something from nothing, ghost seed,
a godless planting, no intent, nothing meant,
just that bursting seed, that rupture,

a splinter of lightning, a following thunder,
and what was born in that lull, a gaping
mouth of the earth, an exhalation from
the depth, where something breathed,

something born, a first birth, an animal,
then another breath, and another, becoming
time, becoming ages and eras, crows darkening
the sky in late afternoon,

a hummingbird shimmering ruby and green
in july light, suspended like a dazzling cross,
sipping at montbretia, nothing religious about
it, just a spirit come to taste the sweetness
of earth, carrying the well of its heart from
bloom to bloom,

and beneath a streetlamp a woman standing
in the rain, berating a spook and calling into
the night, trying to find a way out of her
dishevelled mind, divining a way back,
singing a song of childhood, when girls held
tea parties at tiny tables on the lawn and combed
the hair of their dolls, as if beauty could
forestall anguish.

amadeus

amadeus, he said, but he meant *matador*,
he was dreaming granada, I could tell from
the context, but he knew his music well,
and I thought it was *ave verum* he began
mumbling, though he didn't know latin,
nor would he remember *el cordobés*,
but he had been repeating *sol y sombra*
all afternoon, the sun blistering through
the venetian blind, him having lost faith
as a teenager, he was saying *amadeus*,
though the song was wrong now, something
raunchy with insensible words, *bird is
the word*, perhaps, laughing, he was
laughing, his right hand strumming
invisible chords, or perhaps performing
a veronica.

intervals

you can hear it some quiet nights, out of tune voices,
well one voice, just your voice pitched wrong,
wrong words, wrong sounds, something outside
your intention, that disarray in the next room, just
a step across the sill, on the edge of a dreaming
that has been waiting for you, an exhalation into
the lungs of that other person you will be, out
of time and clumsy-tongued, but no,

not this time, not all the way this night, the dark
keeping the stars lit, the childing dark that has you
shivering almost at the end of yourself, turning and
furrowed, and thinking that theolonius monk guided
his band by dancing, slowly, finding the intervals,
that dance in the corner of the room, face to the wall.

loosening mind

there was a night when someone
whistled, and I caught a childish
glimpse of a shadow at the window,
a deception of moonlight, and
I fell into words,

horses inside sleep, lava dreams,
doors banging in their broken
frames, and the loosening mind
of earthquakes, *ungrund*, losing
my grip,

how often the universe has been
obliterated, with each death tides
and memory halt, the ant and the
grasshopper, sermons and the magic
flute from a green radio.

Emissary

Over 70, on a fine sunny afternoon, sitting on a bench in a cemetery. Well, it's all about location, isn't it. Nothing happens, except
time. Van Gogh's prisoners, in the small courtyard, walking
endlessly in tight circles. Waiting for something, anything, a bolt
of lightning, a tree. Or, a child's call. Waiting for an emissary
with orders to abandon caution, to give us waking dreams in our
doldrums. Someone to take the wrong stance, to look the wrong
way. Someone to walk into the burning house. Like the old man,
who broke a window and reached through the flames to save his
clock. He tore his shirt doing that. In the morning he was sitting
on a tree stump mending it, the scorched clock in the long grass
beside him, ticking. I think I'm remembering that right. It was a
long time ago. It could be a dream but don't tell mother. It will
make her weep.

Pork Pie Hat

A warlock lived at the end of our street. At least we all thought this unshaven old man had to be a warlock. Every child has a house of mystery and fear on their street. The house was unpainted with an unkempt lawn. We called him Ghost, I guess mainly because we rarely caught sight of him. I glimpsed him once through a window at twilight; he was wearing a pork pie hat. I seemed to lose some of my fear when I saw him wearing that hat. One Hallowe'en, on a dare, I was 9 or 10 years old, I slowly walked to his front door and called "trick or treat", knocking softly. I planted my feet, ready to run. When he opened the door, suddenly, his shadow fell over me. He was laughing. I took a step back. He moved forward beneath the porch light. I could see he was wearing his pork pie hat, and a medal glinted on his chest. But what momentarily froze me was his hand reaching toward me. He held a wooden leg, as if he was greeting me with it. I turned and got the hell out of there. I grew older, left home, forgetting the old house and the gaunt man. I was living in the city, years later, when I received a box, and a letter from a lawyer saying I had inherited a pork pie hat from the old man back in my home town. His will said I was the only person who had ever knocked on his door, the hat was mine. It was a strange moment. I put on the hat; it fit perfectly, and I felt a surge of emotion. As if I knew precisely, for the first time, who I was. It wasn't the opera, not Charles Mingus nor Vladimir in Waiting for Godot. It was me, and what I felt was joy. What I felt was love. From whom or for whom I didn't know, and I still don't. I wear the hat to this day, and I understand nothing.

The House

I woke up in a house of ghosts and ladders. It was just a two-storey ramshackle place, but it held a thousand rooms. I was in the basement before a dead furnace. I knew this was the place where children were flayed. The pantry was filled with mostly empty sealer jars, refracting light from a source I couldn't locate. One jar, on a high shelf in front of a 60-watt bulb, held a pear that glowed like a fetus. It felt like someone was in the coal bin, but when I looked there was no one, just a few pieces of coal. I heard faint piano music above me, so I climbed a ladder to the main floor. There was flour on the linoleum and a slumping geranium on a window sill. I walked to another room. I noticed a scurrying in each new room I entered, small wisps of dust at the doorways. The living room was empty except for a stand-up piano. Middle C had been blackened as if someone had put a match to it. I played a chord but there was no sound, the wires had been cut. This was the room of endless practice, rehearsals for perfection. I heard more music, faint and above. I climbed a ladder to the second floor, ending up in the middle of a funeral, so it seemed. My head bumping against the sloped ceiling, I looked around but saw no one at first. It felt like a death, a dirge from somewhere. Then I spotted a plain pine coffin on two sawhorses at the gable end. I walked over to it on a rough plank floor and opened it slowly. There it was, a baby doll, brilliant blue eyes wide open, and fish bones all around.

Hunter's Moon

He walked through the city for three nights; two nights before, and the night of the Hunter's Moon. Each night he met no one, though the streets were lit. No one else walked those nights, and no one smelled his despair. He thought the moon could cleanse him. Or, perhaps, he thought it would take notice and return his lover to him.

Each day, in the heat of day, whether at a café table or in a shop, people felt the despair seeping out of him and threatening to enter them. They avoided him, and conversations were few. He walked all day through the streets, almost as alone as at night. Indeed, he felt more alone than at night.

On the night of the Hunter's Moon, still in despair, his lover lying with another, he turned to darker alleys. Though he met no one, he saw shadows everywhere, in doorways and on dark corners. He walked.

At last, worn, he found the window where his love lay. He stood there, beneath the open shutters, and looked up. From the window came a beautiful voice, a woman singing a song of nightingales. He turned away to go home. But home was everywhere. He sat down on a bench and listened.

Interview

They called him an atheist, but they were interfering with his biography. He hadn't said that at all. In fact, he hadn't said much of anything about it, just that he didn't know. They also said there was really no story. Stories had long worn out, had become advertising. But he had a biography. Maybe it could have been put together differently, that's always true, but it hadn't been so far. A car had backfired in the street, he remembered that. It made him forget the question. It turned out a car hadn't backfired, there'd been a robbery across the way. He didn't remember his answer. Could be that's when he became an atheist. He was thinking about the soundtrack for *The Thin Red Line*, how music growled out of a crocodile's mouth, growing into some kind of dark rapture.

A Kind of Longing

Still looking, he says, but not sure what that is, a kind of longing in itself, not for anything. He says he believes in a lot of things, not at the same time. He needs a belief, hoping that's what he's looking for. They keep piling up. Maybe, he says, one day the pile will hold together and be that something he's looking for. Critical mass, he calls it, the dormant Catholic in him shining through. Critical mass, his latest belief, the Church of Critical Mass sitting at the top of the heap, covering TM and channeling, which reminds him of England and his brief fling with High Church. That was after meditation went south. He could never find the right sound to mull. Always ended up with that adenoidal snore and his lights out, dreaming of tacos. But, the longing never leaves, having become a kind of cynicism, he says, with its own rites and rituals. There may even be a hymnal for it, though singing doesn't come easy.

Belonging

Perhaps life is lived in a face. I've heard that, and it seemed to be true of him. His face held the conflict of belief and experience. There was a grace to that, undercut by anxiety. He seldom spoke. It's been said that words are wind, and he lived on the prairies after all. And, as in prairie skies, clouds sometimes crossed his face suddenly. Perhaps this is what you would expect of a man born out of his mother's death. He read from The Revelations every night, as if it was a place of belonging. In late summer afternoons he stood outside to watch crows flying to their roost. He photographed them with an old Canon, carefully pasting the photos in a black album. During the day he worked with his hands and dreamed of passage. One year, when the weather turned, he built a canoe in the basement, but he never brought it out, for fear of water.

Victoria Creams

She's wanted to leave for a while, having had visits from the dead. Her suitcase, empty in the closet, untouched in years. Each day she mulls in her wheelchair, gazing out the window at frozen patches of brown grass, an emptiness she has always loved, the kind of sparse beauty that gives her room to think. Crows fly by the window. A moment of dark glamour. The sun moves infinitesimally, though it occurs to her that it has probably moved thousands of miles out there in the intensely blue sky, and all she sees is her 94-year-old reflection. What a crow I am, she says aloud, an old crow. The world wrung out with greed and terror. People looking for magic to save them. There is extinction in her face. Wheeling about to find her suitcase, she crams it with photos, a Bible, her diary and letters, and drops it outside the door, a clasp breaking. Let someone else carry the detritus. But she keeps a box of Victoria Creams and cradles it in her lap. Choosing one, she raises it to her mouth, then wheels back to the window where the sun has moved infinitely again. The old woman in the window vanishing in all that vastness. The one thing to take with her, a taste.

After the Last Trick

"Houdini," she said, and paused, looking at him, then struggled for a moment, moving her tongue to shape breath into words. He tried to find the gist within the sounds that seemed to be words and had once been. Moving her papery hand in a dismissive gesture as if waving something away, she made a sound like air escaping from a punctured tire. "After, after," she repeated. He didn't know what she meant, or remembered. It was as if she went from one room to another but forgot why she had gone. She spoke slowly and deliberately. "Nothing left." He nodded, listening, and she continued, "in the grave." She smiled, then leaned toward him and winked. "That trick," she said, turning to look out the window, "after the last trick."

A Childish Moment

Always there are rivers flowing through our stories. I was taught that two and two is four. The cosmos is blowing up forever. An immaculate outward expansion that I can't usually hear. Yet, some days, when I listen, it seems there is an unprogrammed gap, some gasp of mystery or horror, maybe a guffaw; I can hear something. I mean between guffaws. I used to swim in the river of my childhood, then I grew up and left. Now, returning, I find it has dried up. There was a moment, a childish moment, when two and two was five. It was a perfect day. My pantlegs were rolled up, and I was standing in the river. The sun grew hot, my skin was burning, and my eyes went dark. The way music sometimes goes dark, abruptly.

Horizon

It's only horizon, nothing to worry about. The dog will return. And while you're trying to get the car started think about New- love, how dapper he looked with his silver hair and cane. And if you can remember, remind me what year Mantle won the triple crown. Remember listening to the radio, the hum of the crowd, airplanes droning above. You almost felt there in far-off Yankee Stadium. That was before you ran from home. The first time you got to the sea you were disappointed. Too many islands blocked your view. There's always something gets in the way of distance. Even the horizon.

On a Leash

Alone at an outdoor table, slack in the chair, he lay in a smoker's reverie. Smoke curled around the fingers of his left hand which dangled near the ground. His head was tilted back, large sunglasses a wall between his closed eyes and the sun. *How thin the surface of civilization is* was the thought that had come to him as he dreamed a coffee, the café being shuttered because of the contagion. A few minutes earlier a woman had yelled a racial slur at a Chinese girl walking by. She was down the street now, a well-dressed old woman, and her small dog on a leash. There was a lot of that around these days. Fear, then anger, followed closely by hatred. He lifted his hand to take a drag from his cigarette, handling it carefully and gazing at the lengthening ash as it began to droop. It looked like a bridge arching through the air. It reminded him of that small pedestrian bridge across the Darro in Granada. A brick had been missing at the top of the arch. He loved Granada, and he breathed deeply and sighed. Either his sigh, or his trembling hand, dislodged the ash, and it crumbled, falling slowly to the ground.

Despondency

His despondency broke for a moment. It was a despondency of boredom, of nothing happening though a pestilence was moving silently through the world, of losing a sense of who he was. Wondering what he held within himself, what was carried on his breath. And it broke with sudden laughter. He had remembered an image from the previous summer of his wife at a gathering in someone's back yard. From a conversation with a friend he had shifted his gaze over to her. She was almost horizontal in her lawn chair, balancing a glass of wine on her stomach. A drunkard. Without thinking he had laughed then, as he was laughing now. She was nothing of the kind, but the word had seemed to match the image, and probably the unlikeliness of the association was what made him laugh. And now his despondency fragmented in the sound of his growing laughter. The laughter built upon itself and soon brought tears. But he was aware this wouldn't continue, that he would run out of laughter, and despondency would return. The long, long dirt road of despondency and nothing changing, and he laughed harder.

Watching

I heard talk of God but it's nothing I've seen. Sometimes I think it's a hawk, some magnificent raptor. Or, a cage with an open door. But I haven't seen it. When I was a child I thought I did. Or heard it. In the leaves outside my bedroom window, at night, rain or a shivering breeze. But it vanished. Just gone. Like love, you know, in the end. Like anything passing by. I think I saw heaven once, that was in my old man's dying eyes. I could see it there, behind the pain. He had cold hands. My mother used to say "cold hands, warm heart". Not this time. It was a magician's disappearing act, and us unable to imagine it. Standing there, watching, a roomful of nerves waiting on the afterlife.

Gulled

What the sea brings forth, we shall eat, sang a choir of gulls. It sounded almost Biblical, Elizabethan. Them wheeling high and then plummeting to graze shoaling fish. Squabbling and screaming, graceful turns and sudden lifts, with an eye for death. Them singing in tongues, and their grey and white vestments just back from the cleaners. And gathering again for a moment before scattering out to sea or inland, or overhead. *And what passes through us, shall descend upon your streets and your heads*, they scatted. Absolutely the King James Version.

Prodigal

He appeared one morning, like an overnight mushroom, on a leafy street in town. It took some days before people began talking about him. Everyone assumed he was a visitor at one of the houses on that street. The boy was blue-eyed, skinny and barefoot, about 13, and he enjoyed talking with people he met; he didn't make strange. His talk, they said was a little weird as he contradicted himself constantly, even within the same sentence sometimes. "The world is round which is why it's so flat," was one of the things he supposedly said. He even grew a little theological, saying "God is good, so good he's Lucifer." By this time it was clear he belonged to no one in town and didn't appear to even be related to anyone. One man, walking to work early in the morning, claimed he had seen him asleep in a lilac hedge. A woman said she saw evidence of him having made a small fire behind the family garage. She also noted that their cat was missing, but that was not unusual. People began worrying when they caught him peering through their windows at night. Blinds were pulled down and curtains drawn. Still, some claimed to see his shadow through the blinds. Then, gradually, people realized he was gone. The town felt empty, though they were happy to be rid of him. He had been a lurking problem, a possible danger. Stories circulated about him, about the odd things he had said, about his deeds. An announcement was placed in the weekly newspaper asking people to write in if they saw the boy. More and more there were stories of times he had helped people. One man said that he had weeded his garden overnight. Another said that his sick daughter got better when the boy spent the night in their hedge. And once in a while someone would write a letter to the newspaper claiming to have seen the boy, whom they had taken to calling Prodigal, walking down a country road or sitting in a tree at the edge of town. Strange sightings. And, then, there were no more claims, and the boy disappeared from their minds. But, children remembered the stories that had been told to them at bedtime, and when they grew up, and had their own children, they repeated the stories. One story said he had fought bravely in some war. Another said he'd become an alcoholic in the big city, or he was struck down by a car on the highway where, in fact, a shoe was found. But, one argued, he was always barefoot. Another said, no, not always; he had given him a pair of used shoes, and the shoe in the ditch looked exactly like those shoes. And when their children grew up, the stories grew both wilder and wiser. Eventually, town council named a park after the boy. Prodigal Park displayed a bronze plate on a stone telling the story of Prodigal, the boy who could outrun anyone, who collected enough bottles to cash in for a VW car, who had married a beggar's daughter just before he left town. Prodigal had sailed to some third world country, they said, where he became a king. By this time many of the people who had first seen the boy in town were in the cemetery. Life went on, people died and people were born. Sometimes visitors commented on how many children were named Prodigal. This naming had just crept up on the town, everyone thinking they were the only one to name their child Prodigal. Some insisted they named their child after the park, not the boy; others changed their child's name, embarrassed at finding so many Prodigals. Many thought the original Prodigal would return one day and tell them all the adventures he had had out in the world, would have wisdom he could impart. So they believed.

Will-o'-the-Wisp

Gabble, that's what they did. With such enthusiasm and intention, you'd think the world depended on it. Sisters they were, three of them, on a bench in the cemetery. All the others had left, and the casket sat there, suspended above the hole. They spoke quickly, all talking at the same time, interweaving, so that you couldn't make sense of it except for a phrase now and then. Jabbering. One lit a cigarette and carelessly threw the match away; it landed on the pile of dirt beside the grave and slid into the hole. I wondered if it was still burning. The image of that, a small flame in the grave, caught my attention. The other sisters lit their cigarettes from the first one. Gabbling, sucking in smoke quickly between words, and exhaling it along with their incomprehensible words. Yes, I thought, like they have fire in their lungs. My co-worker arrived with two shovels, handed one to me. When I flicked the switch to slowly lower the casket, the three sisters leapt up, heeled their cigarettes and walked to the grave. In unison, they recited, *and I will dwell in the house of the Lord forever.* Heads bowed, they stood wordless. I wondered if that little fire could survive, maybe scorch the wooden casket as it came down. Perhaps, after we filled in the grave, the fire would burn the casket and set the body alight, a ghost of a flame finding its way through the porous earth to flicker above the grave at night. We waited, leaning on our shovels.

Who Can Outlast the Weather?

The bell of Saint Mary's Cathedral woke me where I slept in a desolate hotel. I was no Christian, but that iron ringing had taken me from a dream of thousands of people on their knees in a field. I had no idea what they were doing, but it felt ominous. An old locomotive with steam rising from its stack stood on tracks nearby with a man hammering at a loose spike. The clock radio came on with news of a world-wide plague. I turned it off. Sometimes news is very old. It has happened before. Or, was that a dream as well? A woman dead of the Spanish Flu on her rumpled bed, a baby sucking at her nipple. The screen door wide open and blood on the porch steps, and a pine box. It might have been the weather, but who can outlast the weather?

Gardener

The lank-haired Dutch gardener speaks of beauty. But it's only a word, he says, a meager word. The garden is a promise. He scythes long grass in October, measuring another season. Brown is a colour too, he says, and grey. My father grew vegetables for the family, but he loved his glads more. He had no words, keeping loose sepia photographs of dead relatives in open black coffins at the back of the family photo album. Hidden away and awaiting resurrection. The Dutch gardener is on his knees; he wants to build a wildness into his garden. But architecture fails him again and again. Moriarty used to talk about wildness, its necessity, how he hoped to walk backwards across China before he died. He was a gardener as well, shaping language with his secateurs and soil knife. And, then, one day, abandoning the garden, he left his hair behind for bird nests.

Concert

Every night I went to the concert hall to listen to the orchestra. It didn't matter that it was the same cycle of music being played night after night. There was enough variety to keep my interest going. It moved from the Middle Ages to Mahler, from baroque to Arvo Pärt. This went on for a month. Occasionally one or two musicians were missing. I didn't pay close attention at first, but then noticed those same players weren't returning. Nor were they being replaced. Of course, with time, the sound was affected as more musicians disappeared. This was especially evident when all the percussionists, but one, vanished. And, so, each piece of music began sounding a little different. Thinner, at first, and then silent in certain passages. An effort was made, I noticed, for other instruments to improvise in places where there were no notes for them; they were covering the silence, managing continuity. Within a few weeks some pieces were no longer recognizable; they had become new. The audience was thinning out as well, and those that remained no longer spoke with each other before the concert began or during breaks between pieces. So it went. One evening I arrived to discover I was the only audience member and, on stage, only two remained, a percussionist with his shaker and the conductor. The night after that revealed only the conductor, his arms waving about, his long fingers articulate. The music was familiar, although no one had written it.

Almost in the Same Story

Yes, that is me walking up the stairs. How beautiful she is in her sleep, one leg uncovered in the summer heat, her face astonishingly innocent. That is someone else going down the stairs. And someone else again wandering out the back door to stand in the night. And, history changes. I can hear it, like wings fluttering. Ploughshares and belligerence. Nations. And that is me climbing the stairs. Or, someone like me, someone almost in the same story. She is so beautiful in her vast sleep, her leg tucked in now, her face turned the other way. There are thefts and lies and hunger in the homeless city. Languages crumble. The stories are all shifting, negotiations breaking off. I can sleep in this burning house.

Buson's Bell

He stood still, listening, as if the clarity of the bell opened a fissure in the created world. A moment of emptiness. Between one stroke, with its dying reverberations, and the next, there was a gathering silence that withered into absence. Annihilation. Buson's yellow butterfly lighting on the bell's shoulder.

ACKNOWLEDGEMENTS

These poems were written on the original lands of the Anishinaabeg, Cree, Oji-Cree, Dakota, and Dene peoples in Manitoba, and on the homeland of the Métis Nation in Winnipeg, on the unceded territories of the Musqueam, Squamish and Tsleil-Waututh peoples in Vancouver, of the Tsartlip people in Brentwood Bay, and of the Lekwungen-speaking Songhees and Esquimalt people in Victoria, B.C.

Many of the poems in this collection were previously published in journals and magazines and I would like to thank the editors at the following publications: *Prairie Fire*, *New Quarterly*, *Malahat Review*, *Grain*, *subTerrain*, and *CVII*.

There are many people to thank. Among them are Margie Gillis, Maggie Nagle, Richard Hildebrandt, Esther Warkov, Per Brask, Big Dave McLean, Allan Safarik, and Marilyn Lerner, friends and artists whose work, and dedication to their work, encouraged and influenced me over the years. For my oldest friendship, Ralph Friesen, and friendships since, too numerous to list all, but including Terence and Patricia Young, Bill Gaston and Dede Crane, Michael Elcock and Marilyn Bowering, Maggie Redekop, Maurice Mierau, Victor Enns, Sharon Thesen, Niels Hav, Ulrikka Gernes, Miriam Toews, Peter Feniak, Carol Reid, Chris Welsh, Carol Matas, Derk Wynand, Wendy Atkinson and Van Varga, Paul Tiessen and Hildi Froese Tiessen, John Gould and Sandy Mayzell, Janice McCachen and Pierre MacKenzie, and for inspirational teachers and mentors Dorothy Livesay, P. K. Page, George Amabile, Myron Turner, Mel Toews, Roy Vogt, Lenny Anderson, Victor Cowie and John Moriarty. Always, thank-you to my first and best reader, editor, and partner, Eve Joseph.

And, also, deep appreciation to Marijke Friesen for her book covers, and to Niko Friesen for his music. Thanks to my family, Marijke Friesen, Pedro and Jonah Mendes, Niko Friesen, Jen and Elliot Funo, Leigh Joseph, Lee, Ava and Jake Glazier, Saul Joseph and Katie Dolphin, Salia Joseph and Joe Currie.

I would like to acknowledge my siblings Germaine, Kenton, Kevin and Marcie, and, above all, my mother Margaret Sawatzky Friesen who taught me to read before I got to school, who loved to read stories with me, and talk about them, who wrote poetry Saturday nights as she looked out the picture window at snowy fields, who had an insatiable curiosity and adventurousness, keeping the girl in her alive. Thanks to my grandfather, Jacob Sawatzky, a most generous, unjudging man with a wonderful sense of humour, and to my great-grandmother Anna Sawatzky, from whom all this may have flowed.

Appreciation to Brian Kaufman and Karen Green of Anvil Press for their generous support and enthusiasm for this book, and just for the marvelous work they, and many others, do as small press publishers.

Remembering Joe Rosenblatt, Jim Donahue, Andris Taskans, Jake MacDonald, Patrick Lane and Eva Wynand.

Thank-you to the BC Arts Council for financial aid in the writing of the new poems at the end of this book, and for previous aid as well, and to Canada Council for aid at two or three different times during the writing of these poems.

PERMISSIONS

The selected poems from the following volumes were reprinted with the permission of the publishers. We thank them for their generosity.

A Broken Bowl, Brick Books, 1997, www.brickbooks.ca

st. mary at main, The Muses' Company, 1998, www.jgshillingford.com

the breath you take from the lord, Harbour Publishing, 2002, www.harbourpublishing.com

Earth's Crude Gravities, Harbour Publishing, 2007, www.harbourpublishing.com

jumping in the asylum, Quattro Books, 2011, www.quattrobooks.ca

a dark boat, Anvil Press, 2012, www.anvilpress.com

a short history of crazy bone, Mother Tongue Publishing, 2015, www.mothertonguepublishing.com

songen, Mother Tongue Publishing, 2018, www.mothertonguepublishing.com